Successf

G000140027

"Successful Running involves the improvement of personal performance whilst respecting individual biology."

B. Petračić/ F.-J. Röttgermann/ K.-Ch. Traenckner

Successful Running
The Medical and Biological
Background to Improved Performance

Meyer & Meyer Sport

Original title: Optimiertes Laufen
- Aachen : Meyer & Meyer Verlag, 1997
Translated by Paula Radcliffe

British Library Cataloguing in Publication Data
A catalogue record for this book is available from the British Library

Petracic, Bozo:
Successful Running :The Medical and Biological Background to Improved Performance /
Bozo Petracic/Franz-Joachim Röttgermann/Kurt-Christian Traenckner.
- Oxford : Meyer & Meyer Sport (UK) Ltd., 1999
ISBN 1-84126-006-1

© 1999 by Meyer & Meyer Sport (UK) Ltd.
Oxford, Aachen, Olten (CH), Vienna, Québec, Lansing/Michigan,
Adelaide, Auckland, Johannesburg, Budapest
Graphics: Diag. 1, 2, 4-10 after: Kapandji, Enke Verlag;
Diag. 84-92 after: Spring et al., Georg-Thieme-Verlag;
164, 166 after: de Marées, Sport & Buch Strauß GmbH;
165 after: Aschoff, Urban & Schwarzenberg Verlag;
169, 170 after: Verlag Europa Lehrmittel;
171, 172 after: Hoechst Trevira KG, Frankfurt/Main;
167, 173 after: Mecheels, Verlag Schiele & Schön GmbH;
175-177, Tab. 5, example 1+2 after: Verein der Sportärzte Oberhausen;
178-180 after: Polar Electro GmbH, Büttelborn;
all others after: Artoon Studios, Bernd Jünger & Annette Beyß, Aachen
Lithos: S. 84, 85, 87, 88, 94, 96-98/ Exposure: frw, Reiner Wahlen, Aachen
Photos: Franz-Joachim Röttgermann, Oberhausen
Cover Photo: Polar Electro GmbH, Büttelborn
Cover design: Birgit Engelen, Stolberg
Cover exposure: frw, Rainer Wahlen, Aachen
Editorial: John Coghlan; Dr. Irmgard Jaeger, Aachen
Type: Quay
Printed and bound in Germany by Druckpunkt Offset GmbH,
ISBN 1-84126–006-1
e-mail: verlag@meyer-meyer-sports.com

Contents

I   Introduction

Whether we like it or not, the stresses and strains of everyday life frequently put our bodies under pressure. According to their heart/circulation, muscular and bone structure, and even their psychological make-up, each individual has a differing ability to cope with the burden. As long as the stress and the ability to cope with this strain remain fairly equal the individual has no problems: he feels fit and healthy. By taking part in sport we place ourselves under greater pressure, which brings us as near as possible to our personal resilience limit. However, this limit is not fixed, it is dependant to a certain extent on the type of stress and can be extended within certain limits.

This is achieved through specific and systematic training – although the effects will not be immediately noticeable – and our resilience must be stimulated in certain ways. For example, if the endurance training load is too low then the individual resilience will decrease over time and the desired effect will not be achieved. However, if we train in harmony with our abilities then we will fully bid up our possibilities so that resilience will slowly, but surely, increase.

This improvement can only be plotted as far as an individual threshold. The resilience of an individual sports person is determined by limiting biological factors, such as age and anatomical shortcomings. In sport, if biological limits are not observed, this can lead to an overburdening, which brings many unpleasant consequences. The first signs of overburdening do not necessarily mean illness. However, this can result, if the athlete does not recognise and alleviate the causes of the overburdening quickly enough, in irreparable damage to their health thus bringing their sporting career to a premature end.

The authors of this book have set themselves the task of providing long-distance runners and joggers, both male and female top achieving athletes and also those for whom sport is a hobby, with medical knowledge to improve performance and to understand their bodies. Hence athletes will be alerted to overburdening problems and warned of factors damaging to their health. In this way they can target the best possible achievement without impairing their long-term health.

For the athlete, "Optimise Your Running" means getting the most from their bodies while respecting individual limits. Aside from a few exceptions in high achievers, sport should not be a be all and end all, but rather an exclusive means of maintaining health, improving physical well-being and improving quality of life. Thus the athlete needs to choose a training schedule conforming to his needs, running shoes which match his weight and an appropriate balance of mileage and quality in training, as well as eventually checking for orthopaedic weaknesses which need to be corrected. An athlete should know the thermoregulation of his body well enough to understand which clothes protect his body best in which weather conditions, whilst not reducing performance.

Furthermore, when one day an overburdening problem does occur the athlete can react in time, modify the training to the altered biological circumstances and include different sport disciplines in the programme. In this way physical condition is maintained until the temporary problem is overcome.

II The Anatomy and Biomechanics of Running

In order to tailor sports training to suit biological parameters it is imperative to fully understand the effects of running on the suffering muscles and joints, heart and circulation.

1. Effects on the Foot and Ankle Joints

The anatomical structure of the foot is determined by three support arches, two running length ways and one width ways. In this way three points withstand the maximal strain on the foot whilst standing:
On the heel and the head of the first and fifth metatarsals which are linked together through this triangular arches. (Diags. 1+2)

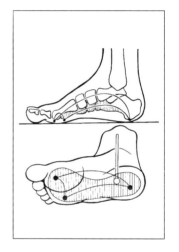

Diags. 1+2:
All three feet supports form a triangle and act as elasticated stays for the foot. (From I. A. Kapandji: "Funktionelle Anatomie der Gelenke", Bd. 2: "Untere Extremitäten", Enke Verlag Stuttgart 1985 (originally published by Editions Maloine, Paris)

These three feet supports are elastically stabilised by bracing bands (passive) and tensing the muscles of the foot and lower leg (active). (Diag. 3)

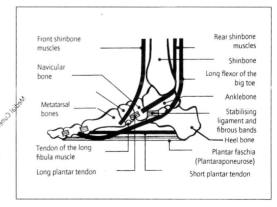

Front shinbone muscles
Navicular bone
Metatarsal bones
Tendon of the long fibula muscle
Long plantar tendon

Rear shinbone muscles
Shinbone
Long flexor of the big toe
Anklebone
Stabilising ligament and fibrous bands
Heel bone
Plantar faschia (Plantaraponeurose)
Short plantar tendon

Diag. 3:
Active and passive bracing of the bone structure in the foot

This anatomical structure enables the foot to absorb the impact caused by walking and running on hard surfaces, otherwise impacted fully on the ankle, knee and hip joints as well as on the spinal column.

The movements of the foot, the standing leg, plotted by **Kapandji** in four steps.

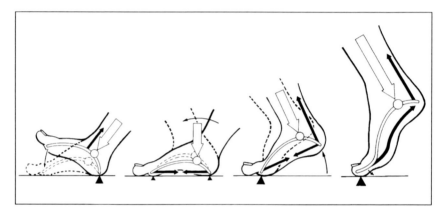

Diag. 4-7:
From I. A. Kapandji: "Funktionelle Anatomie der Gelenke", Bd. 2: "Untere Extremitäten", Enke Verlag Stuttgart 1985 (originally published by Editions Maloine Paris)

Phase 1:
Heel contact with the ground
(landing phase)

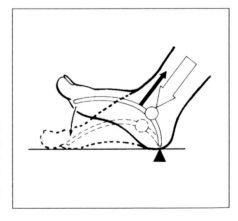

Foot is pulled up from the neutral position of the ankle joint by tensing the muscles of the lower leg, which lever the foot (black arrow). The foot makes contact with the ground at the heel. Shortly after the weight of the runner is directed through the lower leg (white arrow) to force the whole sole of the foot to the ground.

Phase 2:
Contact between the sole of the foot and the ground (rolling phase)

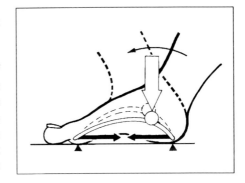

The weight is absorbed by the arch of the foot as it flattens itself. This flattening of the long arch is controlled by the elastic tension of the foot ligaments (passive) and the contraction of the short underfoot muscles on the sole (active) to produce a shock absorption effect.

Phase 3:
Heel take-off (1ˢᵗ push off phase)

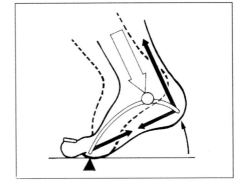

The long arch of the foot is lifted by actively straining the short underfoot muscles. At the same time the calf muscles contract to put upward tension through the Achilles' tendon and lift the heel. The forefoot is strongly loaded and widened by the flattening of the crossways arch.

Phase 4:
Take-off phase (2ⁿᵈ push off phase)

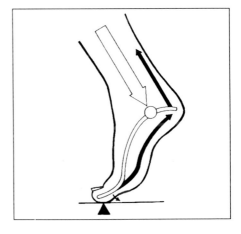

The weight transfers from the forefoot through the ball onto the toes, which brace themselves accordingly. The crossways arch of the foot rises. Through a strong contraction of the calf, short underfoot and toe flexor muscles the body is pushed forward and the foot lifted. The standing leg becomes the moving leg and the other leg undertakes the functions of the standing leg.

These movement phases of the foot occur only with so-called heel-strike runners. With mid-foot strikers the first contact between the standing leg and the ground occurs at the ball of the foot and only the two latter phases are followed. The muscles used in this phase are put under greater strain than those of a heel-strike runner.

Metaphorically, one can divide the ankle joint into two functions, an upper (lifting and lowering of the foot) and lower (controlling the foot by way of supination or pronation).

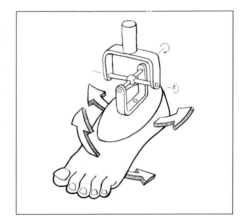

Diag. 8:
The upper (lowering/raising of the foot) and lower ankle joint (supination/ pronation) both work according to the universal joint principle. (From I. A. Kapandji: "Funktionelle Anatomie der Gelenke", Bd. 2: "Untere Extremitäten", Enke Verlag Stuttgart 1985 (originally published by Editions Maloine, Paris)

In the landing phase of running the lower ankle joint is in a state of mild supination. In the rolling phase it takes on a neutral position, and in the take-off phase it increasingly adapts into a position of pronation. (Diag. 9)

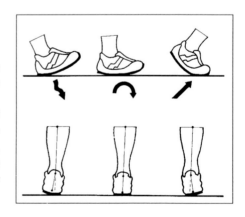

Diag. 9:
Position of the upper and lower ankle joints in different phases of running: landing, rolling, and take-off phase. Right foot shown from the outside and from behind. (From I. A. Kapandji: "Funktionelle Anatomie der Gelenke", Bd. 2: "Untere Extremitäten", Enke Verlag Stuttgart 1985 (originally published by Editions Maloine, Paris)

2. Effects on the Knee and Upper Leg Muscles

The knee is not only a hinge which enables the leg to bend and stretch through a rolling/sliding movement, it also allows an additional rotational movement of the lower leg in relation to the upper leg. Diag.10, see chpt. IV.

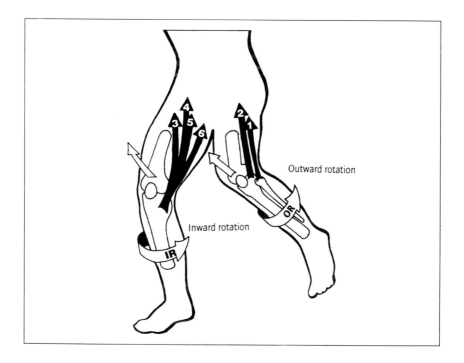

Diag. 10:
The bending and stretching scope of the knee joint might be broadened further by the rotational movement. The adductors function as inward rotators of the lower leg: sartorius muscle (3), semitendinosus muscle (4), semimembranosus muscle (5) (collectively known as the harmstrings), musculus gracilis (6). The lateral thigh muscles control the outward rotation: biceps femoris (1), tensor fasciae latae (2).
(From I. A. Kapandji: "Funktionelle Anatomie der Gelenke", Bd. 2: "Untere Extremitäten", Enke Verlag Stuttgart 1985 (originally published by Editions Maloine Paris)

Demands placed on the muscle groups and effects on the knee during different phases of running: (standing leg)

Diag. 11:

Knee:	Up to five times body weight.	3-5 times body weight.	Relaxed.
Patella:	Relaxed.	Up to ten times static pressure.	Three times static pressure.
Liga-ments:	Side ligaments and front crucial ligament under tension.	Relaxed.	Side ligaments and front crucial ligament under tension.
Muscles and tendons:	M. rectus femoris, M. iliopsoas, tractus ido tibialis, Adductors/foot lifters in use.	M. quadrizeps, tractus iliotibialis Adductors in use.	Thigh flexors, gluteal muscle M. popliteus, calf muscle and Achilles' tendon, short underfoot muscles in use.

Demands placed on the muscle groups and the effects on the knee during different phases of running: (moving leg)

Diag. 12:

Knee:	Relaxed.	Relaxed.	Relaxed.
Patella:	Twice static pressure.	2-3 times static pressure.	Three times static pressure.
Liga-ments:	Rear crucial ligament and side ligaments under tension.	Rear crucial ligaments and side ligaments under tension.	Rear crucial ligaments and side ligaments under tension.
Muscles and tendons:	Gluteal muscle M. gluteus thigh flexors M. biceps femoris, M. semimembranosus M. semitendineus in use.	Gluteal and thigh flexor muscles. in use.	Thigh flexors M. iliopsoas, M. rectus femoris, M. tensor fasciae latae in use.

When the knee joint bends and stretches the kneecap (patella) glides up and down between the femur rolls. When the knee is bent and the thigh muscles tensed, the force exerted by the kneecap on the sliding area on the femur, is up to ten times higher, and the strain on the patella tendon is increased. (Diag. 13)

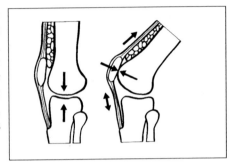

Diag. 13:
When the knee bends and the thigh muscle (M. quadriceps) tenses, the pressure on the kneecap increases and a strain is enforced on the patella tendon.

The knee is stabilised passively by the side and crucial ligaments and actively through the contraction of the thigh muscle. Between 20 and 60 degrees of knee flexion all ligaments are relaxed and only the muscles and their tendons (M. quadriceps with patella tendon, M. tensor fasciae latae with tractus iliotibialis and the tendons of the adductor muscles) are working to stabilise. (Diags. 14-16)

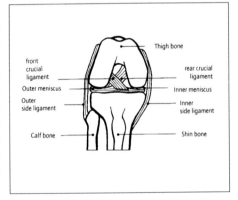

Diag.14:

The side and crucial ligaments and the menisci work as passive stabilisers of the knee joint.

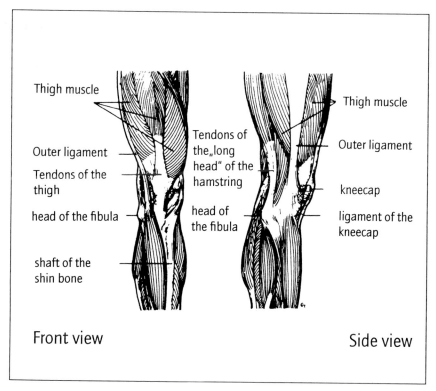

Thigh muscle

Outer ligament

Tendons of the thigh

head of the fibula

shaft of the shin bone

Tendons of the „long head" of the hamstring

head of the fibula

Thigh muscle

Outer ligament

kneecap

ligament of the kneecap

Front view

Side view

Diags. 15+16:
The thigh muscles is an active stabiliser of the knee.
Diag. 15: Front view
Diag. 16: Side view

During running the knee joint and the thigh muscles are put under extreme pressure. Of all the joints in our bodies the knee comes under the most pressure and is greatly at risk from injury and overloading. In the landing phase of running, five times our weight passes through the knee joint, and in the rolling stage the thigh muscles (M. quadriceps) must absorb 3-4 times weight. The strain on the kneecap can increase up to ten times and accordingly the pull on the patella tendon augments. The demands of the muscles and effects on the knee during different phases of running are shown for both the standing and moving leg in diagrams 11 + 12.

3.   Effects on the Pelvis and Spinal Column

The movement of the trunk during running causes the whole pelvis to pull sidewards on the lumbar vertebrae, and the action of changing leg causes an additional swinging movement. The major twisting point for the pelvis is at the transition from the lumbar vertebrae to the sacrum (lumbosacral transition, also known as a trouble spot of lumbar vertebrae complaints). In addition the junctions of the ilium and the sacrum (ileosacral joint) also come under strong pressure. (Diag. 17)

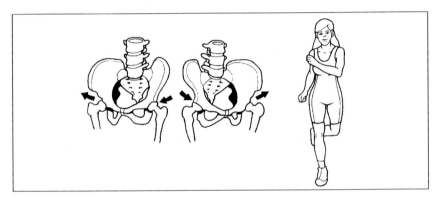

Diag. 17:
Horizontal movements of the pelvis and the vertebrae during running

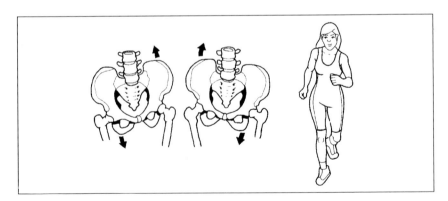

Diag. 18:
Vertical movement of the pelvis and vertebrae (from D. M. Brody)

Running up and down impacts extreme strain on the pelvis and lumbar vertebrae. When running uphill the front section of the lumbar vertebrae and the discs are put under increased pressure. When running downhill the rear sections of the vertebrae, discs and vertebrae joints are greatly stressed. (Diag. 19)

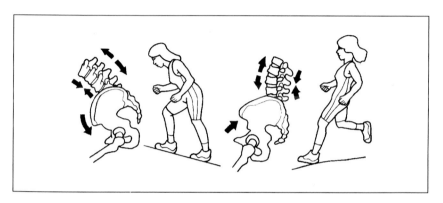

Diag. 19:
Position of the pelvis and lumbar vertebrae during uphill and downhill running (from D. M. Brody)

III. Performance Limiting Biological Conditions

(Self-diagnosis and Preventative Measures)

Inherent or short-term anatomical deviations from the norm cause different tensions in the tendons and muscles, hence an atypically biomechanical style of running with increased risk of overuse problems. The most common performance limiting biological conditions are listed below:

1. Hollow Back (Hyperlordosis of the Lumbar Vertebrae)

1.1 Terms and Biomechanics

By hollow back we mean a marked inward curve, over and above the normal curvature of the spine. Hollow back can occur inherently, or develop through incorrect posture or carriage. Often people with sedentary jobs tend to be susceptible to a shortening of the thigh and hip flexor muscles (M. rectus femoris, M. iliopsoas). As a result of this shortening the hip joint becomes less flexible. As the leg is stretched during running, the decreased flexion of the hip joint and the strain on the shortened muscles lead to a tilting forward of the pelvis thus causing a hollow back. (Diag. 20)

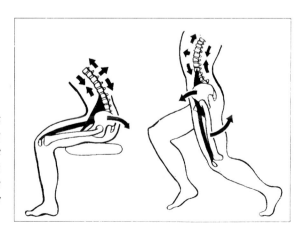

Diag. 20:
The shortened flexor muscles of the thigh cause a tilting of the pelvis forward as the leg is stretched, which bends the lumbar vertebrae into a hyperlordosis (hollow back).

1.2   Diagnosis

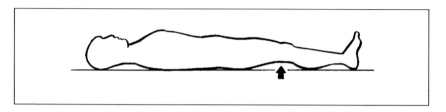

Diag. 21:
Normally there is no gap between the back and the floor.
When the muscles are shortened and the lumbar vertebrae are in contact with the ground there is a gap between the back of the knees and the ground, due to the hip joint adopting a bent position.

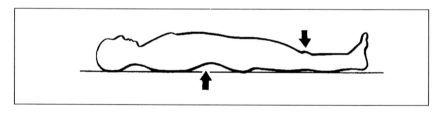

Diag. 22:
When lying relaxed on the back on flat, hard ground with outstretched legs and knees pressed to the ground, individuals with hollow back will have enough space between the lumbar vertebrae and the ground to pass a hand or fist.

1.3   Procedures
Lengthening exercises for the shortened muscles (s. chapter III. 9),
Strengthening of the back muscles (s. chapter IV. 1),
Change of sport (s. chapter IV. 17).

2. Pelvic Misalignment and Leg Length Discrepancies

2.1 Terms and Biomechanics

Leg length discrepancy is rarely caused by a true shortening of one leg (due to an accident, underdevelopment as a child). More often it is the result of a distortion of the pelvis. Pelvic misalignment frequently leads to a sidewards curve of the vertebrae (skoliosis) and an asymmetrical loading of the legs and trunk. The adductor muscles of the shorter leg shorten and the trunk muscles on the same side shrivel. This causes an asymmetrical movement when running. (Diag. 23)

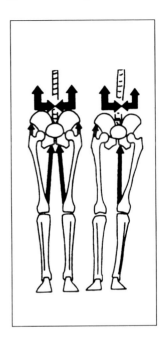

Diag. 23:
A pelvic misalignment with leg length discrepancy causes an asymmetrical loading of the muscles and a shortening of the adductors on the side of the shorter leg.

2.2 Diagnosis

Diag. 24:
When lying relaxed on the back with legs outstretched alongside each other, the inner anklebones should be at one level. If the inner anklebones lie at different heights then a leg length discrepancy exists.

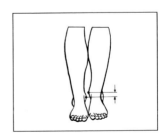

2.3 Procedures

Equalling of the leg length difference (s. chapter V 2.4).
Back exercises. Lengthening exercises for the shorter leg and strengthening of the underdeveloped trunk and leg muscles. A course of physiotherapy and consultation with a sports or orthopaedic doctor is recommended. Afterwards running technique should be corrected.

3.   Hip Misalignment

3.1   Terms and Biomechanics

The hip joint is a ball and socket joint that also determines the rotational position of the leg. In the supine position with outstretched legs the feet should point straight up, unless the thigh muscle is totally relaxed, in which case they have a slight outwards rotation of about 20 degrees. A poorly rotating hip joint can either be caused by shortened muscles or be brought about by the inherent wrong positioning of the head of the femur as it fits into the hip socket. Due to this the biomechanics of running is also altered. (Diags. 25-27) The poor rotation can arise on one or both sides.

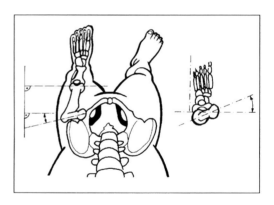

Diag. 25:
The normal angle between the neck of the femur and the diagonal axis of the ball of the femur at the knee is 20 degrees ante version. Normal biomechanics of running is ensured (s. chapter II).

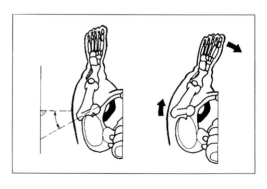

Diag. 26:
An anteversion of the neck of the femur of more than 20 degrees causes an inwards rotation of the feet. The result is a shortening of the inward rotators of the hip joint and a limited degree of outward rotation for the leg.

Diag. 27:
In the case of retroversion of the neck of the femur, the foot takes on an outwardly rotated position. The outward rotators are shortened and the ability of the leg to rotate inwardly is reduced.
Through this the biomechanics of running are also altered: The foot is turned outwards as it is planted and rolls inward.

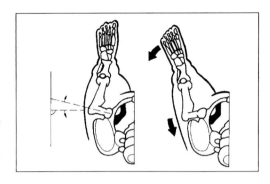

3.2 Diagnosis

A rotational misplacement of the leg (foot) can be recognised by analysing the individual footprints. (Diags. 28 a,b,c)

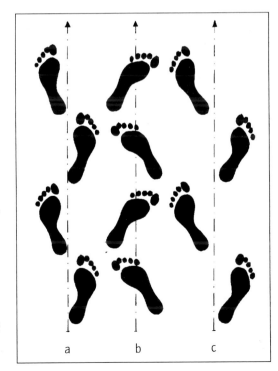

Diag. 28 a:
Impression when positioned normally.

Diag. 28 b:
Inwardly rotated misplacement.

Diag. 28 c:
Outwardly rotated misplacement of the feet.

a   b   c

3.3 Procedures

If the rotational misplacement is caused purely by muscular problems then a specific training programme with stretching exercises usually brings satisfactory results. In the case of morphological causes these can only influence the shortened muscles (physiotherapy). If, in spite of the directed exercises to improve the flexibility of the muscles, problems still occur while running, the only alternative left is to change sports. A prior consultation with an orthopaedic or sports doctor is recommended.

4.   X- and O-Legs

4.1   Terms and Biomechanics

The term X- or O-legs (knee) is used when the loading axis while standing does not run centrally through the knee, but rather passes to the outside (X) or to the inside (O). (Diags. 29-31) Due to this, running or walking places a strain not only on the knee, but also on the ankle joint and the likelihood of overburdening problems is increased.

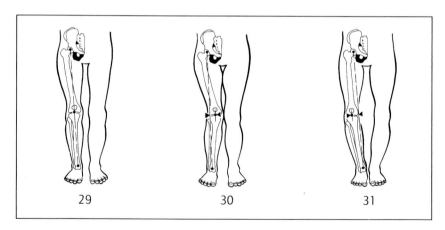

29   30   31

Diags. 29-31:
During normal loading of the legs the loading axis passes from the head of the femur centrally through the knee joint to the middle of the ankle joint (29). In the case of X-legs the loading axis is transferred to the outer side of the knee joint (30) and with O-legs to the inner side (31). As a result the cartilage and the meniscus of the loaded side are overstressed.

4.2 Diagnosis

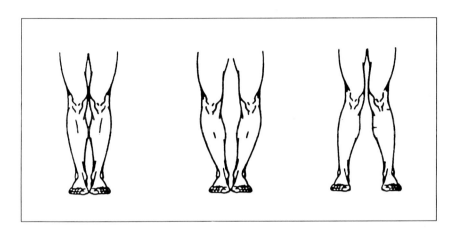

Diag. 32:
When standing straight, with well-developed lateral muscles, the legs come into contact with each other in the thigh area, at the knee joint, at the widest part of the calves and at the inner ankle bones. If both inner ankle bones come together when standing with legs together and there is a gap between the knee joints, then it is a case of O-legs. If both knee joints come together and the inner ankle bones and feet stand apart, then it is a case of X-legs.

4.3 Procedures

The strain on the feet can be largely alleviated by the correct choice of shoes or corrective inserts. (s. chapter V.2)

With more pronounced knee misplacement a corrective operation should be considered, because wrongly loading the knee joint can cause premature wear and tear (arthrosis). A specialist doctor should be consulted.

5.   Divergence of the Kneecap (Lateralisation of the Patella)

5.1   Terms and Biomechanics

When the knee joint bends and stretches, the patella slides in the groove between the two femoral rollers. Thus when the knee is bent the strain of the kneecap is divided between the two femoral rollers. If the shape of the kneecap is such that it only comes into contact with the outer side of the femoral groove, then only this part of the groove will come under the increased strain from the kneecap. This can lead to over-burdening problems. (Diag. 33)

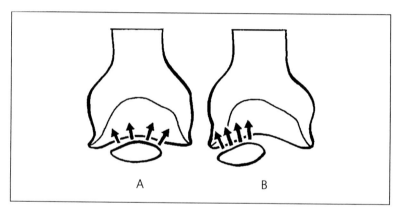

Diag. 33:
A: Normal position of the kneecap in the femoral groove.
B: Lateralised patella with increased strain on the surface of the joint where it comes into contact.

5.2   Diagnosis

Diag. 34:
The sidewards position of the kneecap is best recognised by looking at the front of the knee when bent, for example when sitting with muscles relaxed.

5.3   Procedures

Since lateralisation of the patella usually means that the inner thigh muscle (M. vastus medialis) is underdeveloped, an exercise programme targeted at strengthening this muscle to improve the inward pull on the kneecap is advised.

6.   Misalignment of the Ankle Joint (Hyperpronation, Hypersupination)

6.1   Terms and Biomechanics

The misalignment of the foot at the lower ankle joint in type O (supination) or X (pronation) is often linked to other feet deformities. It can arise on one or both sides and can be inherent or occur later in life. Often it is a consequence of a pronounced flattening of the long arch of the foot. This also alters the direction of the Achilles' tendon and the rolling of the foot is worsened, leading to overburdening problems. If the outer ligaments of the ankle are damaged or weak then there is a tendency to twist the foot inwards (hypersupination).

6.2   Diagnosis

Diag. 35:   *Diag. 36:*
Pronation position   Supination position

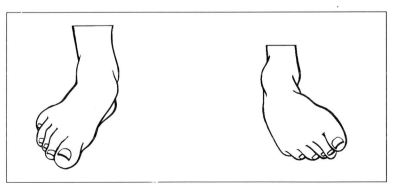

Diag. 37:
A broader foot imprint and an altered angle between the lower leg and heel hyperpronation causes the Achilles' tendon to change position.

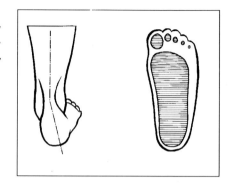

Diag. 38:
In the case of supination the outer edge of the heel and sole of the foot take the impact. The angle between the heel and lower leg opens inwardly, putting the Achilles' tendon into the wrong position. The impression of the foot shows how the pressure is exerted along the outer edge of the foot.

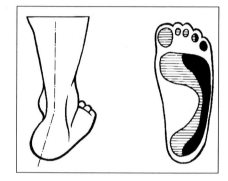

6.3   Procedures

A large proportion of incorrect foot plants can be balanced through the correct choice and design of running shoes. (Diag. 39)

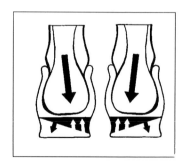

Diag. 39:
The pronation support is a support on the inside of the foot bed which should prevent hyperpronation.

7.   Feet Deformities
(Fallen Arches, Flat-, Splay-, Club- and Hollow Foot)

7.1   Terms and Biomechanics

The popular term flat feet is a collective term for the flattening of the long arch of the foot (fallen arch, Diag. 40) and the dropping of the crossways arch (splayfoot, Diag. 43) both of which involve a widening of the midfoot. These two deformities can often occur together.

When a hyperpronation of the ankle joint also occurs, the condition is widely known as clubfoot. (Diag. 42) In this situation the hard impact in the landing and rolling phases of running is insufficiently neutralised (inadequate shock absorption effect) and the force of landing carries on up the body at full strength.

Hollow foot is an inherent deformity often linked to a raised long arch, high instep, overstretched toes, a shortening of the tendons which straighten the foot and hammer toes. This deformity usually goes together with hypersupination.

In the rolling phase of running, the foot rolls on the outer edge of the sole and the balls of the toes take an extreme impact, giving a tendency towards the build-up of calluses. The second stage of push off is weakened through reduced flexibility of the toes.

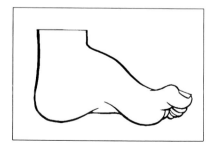

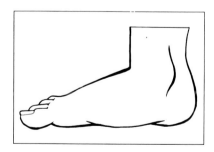

Diag. 40:
Fallen arch

Diag. 41:
Hollow foot

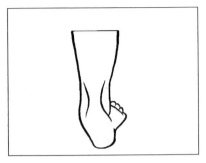

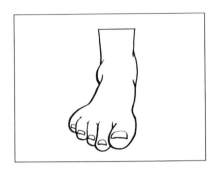

Diag. 42:
Clubfoot

Diag. 43:
Splayfoot

7.2 Diagnosis

Feet deformities and abnormal foot plants can be diagnosed by taking impressions of the feet when running and standing. (Diag. 44) In addition a treadmill analysis is also recommended. (see chpt. V, 2.2)

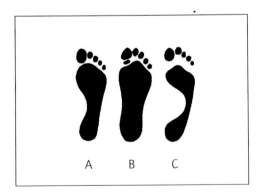

Diag. 44:
A: Impression of a normal foot
B: Impression of a flat foot
C: Impression of hollow foot

7.3 Procedures

Try different anatomical shoe inlays and running shoes, made or adjusted specially by sports orthopaedic shoemakers. (s. chpt. V, 2)

8. Toe Deformities
Crooked and stiff toe (hallux valgus and hallux limitus, hallux rigidus, hammer toe, misrotation of the little toes)

8.1 Terms and Biomechanics

A crooked toe is not just an inherent deformity, it can also be caused by wearing ill-fitting or unsuitable shoes. (Diag. 45) This latter applies more to women than men. As a consequence, the rolling phase of running is shortened and the second take-off phase is not carried out.

In the case of stiff toe, the flexibility of the joint at the base of the big toe is limited. Thus the foot can only roll with difficulty. This limitation is usually caused by a shortening of the long flexor of the big toe.

With hallux rigidus, changes in the joints generally cause painful limitation in the movement of the joint at the base of the big toe. (Diag. 46-47)

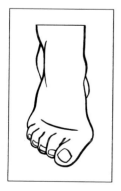
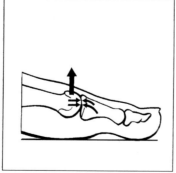
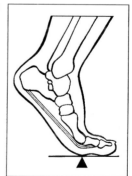

Diag. 45:
Hallux valgus

Diags. 46-47:
Overburdening of hallux limitus and rigidus as the forefoot rolls, especially in the take-off phase (from Marcinko).

8.2   Diagnosis

In the case of a stiff toe the flexibility in both joints of the big toe should be checked. The same method can be used to check for shortening of the toe flexors and thus to diagnose hammer toe.

8.3   Procedures

Less severe cases of toe deformities can be corrected through good running shoes or those specially ordered from orthopaedic shoemakers. With more pronounced problems, which cause significant pain, corrective operations can be very successful. A specialist doctor should be consulted.

Hammer toes or claw toes arise in the course of everyday life as the toe flexors shorten. Corns, or the build-up of calluses on the upper sides of the middle toe joints, are the result of wearing shoes which are too narrow. This can also cause huge problems for runners. This deformity is often associated with hollow foot problems. (Diag. 49)

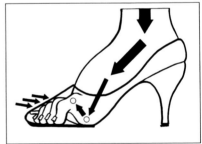

Diag. 48:
The wrong shoe facilitates the forming of hammer toes.

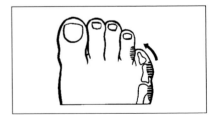

Diag. 49:
With hammer toes the pressure of the shoe causes calluses to build up on the middle toe joints.

Diag. 50:
A twisted little toe gives a tendency towards painful pressure points and blood blisters on the outside of the foot.

9. Shortening of the Muscles and Tendons

9.1 Hip Flexor

9.1.1 Terms and Biomechanics

The strongest flexor of the hip joint is made up in two parts: groin and loin muscles, which attach with the same tendon onto the inner side of the femur. (Diag. 51)

The shortened flexor muscles inhibit the flexibility of the hip joint. In the take-off phase of running the standing leg is stretched maximally at the hip. An incomplete stretch at the hip causes a pull on the muscles of the lumbar vertebrae, which form a hollow back to balance this.

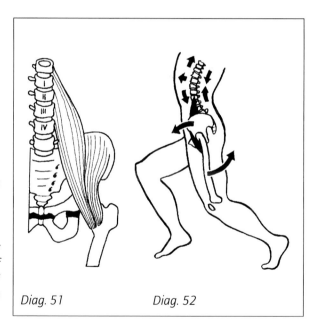

Diag. 51:
Diagram of the hip flexor

Diag. 52:
Insufficient flexibility through shortening of the hip flexor is balanced by a tilting of the pelvis and hollow back.

Diag. 51   *Diag. 52*

A shortening of the muscles on one or both sides brings about reduced mobility in one or more of the joints. An increased pull on the tendons, or on the attachments to the bone, can irritate the surface of the bone and thus cause problems. Since most problems in runners arise through shortened leg or pelvic muscles, the most important muscle groups and their effects for running are listed:

9.1.2   Diagnosis

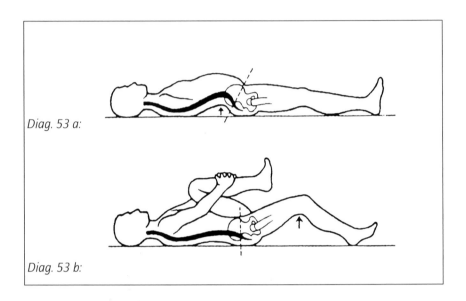

Diag. 53 a:

Diag. 53 b:

Diag. 53a:
Hollow back and a tilted pelvis give a false impression of hip flexibility.

Diag. 53b:
By fully bending the opposite leg to that being tested, hyperlordosis of the lumbar vertebrae and tilted pelvis are blocked. In the case of shortened flexors the leg being tested cannot lie flat with the knee straight.

9.1.3   Procedures

A shortening of the hip flexors can be overcome through a specific stretching programme. In order to prevent a hollow back using exercises to improve hip flexibility, a tilted pelvis should be blocked by maximally bending the other leg. (Diag. 54-55)

Diag. 54:
Correct! Fully bending the left leg blocks a tilted pelvis and a hollow back from forming and thus stretches the hip flexor only.

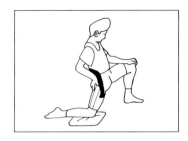

Diag. 55:
Wrong! The stretch of the hip will be achieved through a hollow back forming and the pelvis tilting. This gives only a minimal stretch for the hip flexor.

9.2   Knee Extensor

9.2.1   Terms and Biomechanics

M. rectus femoris is the most important part of the four-part thigh muscle (M. quadriceps) and is responsible for the bending of the knee joint. At the same time it also acts as a hip flexor. (Diag. 56)

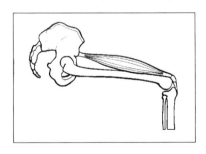

Diag. 56:

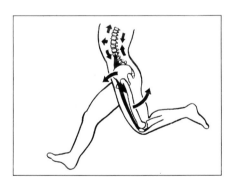

Diag. 57:

The maximal stretching of the muscles whilst running is achieved by bending the knee and stretching the hip of the moving leg.
In the case of shortened muscles, either the capacity of movement of the leg in motion is shortened or the pelvis tilts causing a hollow back to form.

9.2.2   Diagnosis

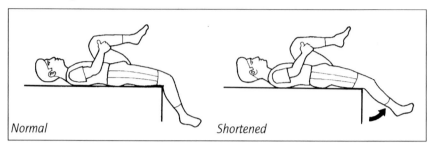

Normal   Shortened

Diag. 58-59:
If M. rectus femoris is shortened the test leg cannot be bent at right angles against the edge of the couch. The lower leg hangs out from the couch according to the extent of the muscle shortening.

9.2.3   Procedures

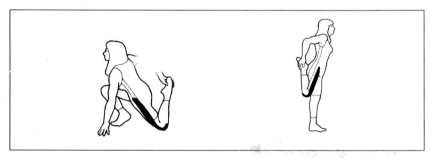

Diag. 60:
Stretching exercises having a strong stretching effect without using the lumbar vertebrae.

Diag. 61:
A good stretch with justifiable loading of the lumbar vertebrae (hollow back).

Diag. 62:
Carrying out the exercises wrongly because heavier loading of the lumbar vertebrae (hollow back) causes pronounced tilting of the pelvis and overburdening of the lumbo-sacral junctures.

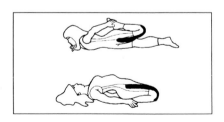

9.3   The Hamstring Muscles
(semitendinosus, semimembranosus, biceps femoris)

9.3.1   Terms and Biomechanics

The hamstring muscles link the pelvic girdle with the back of the shin bone and control the bending of the knee. (Diag. 63) The maximal stretch on these muscles occurs in the landing phase of running as the standing leg straightens.

A shortening of the hamstring muscles inhibits the full stretching of the lower limb, which can result in the pelvis tilting backwards, thus flattening the normal curve of the lumbar vertebra resulting in more wear and tear on the front of the individual vertebra and the discs. (Diag. 63)

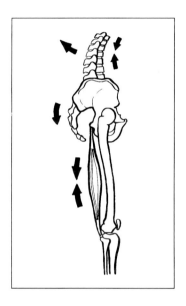

Diag. 63:
How the hamstring muscles work and the effects of a shortening on the vertebrae.

9.3.2   Diagnosis

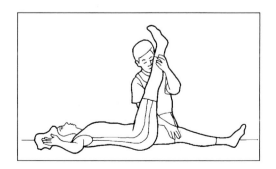

Diag. 64:
When lying on the back the leg can normally be raised with the knee outstretched to make an angle of 80-90 degrees with the ground.

Diag. 65:
With reduced flexibility, due to
shortened muscles, the angle
with the ground is less.

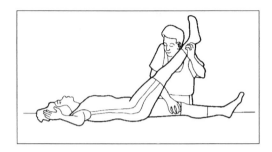

9.3.3 Procedures

The flexibility of the hamstring muscles can be improved by carrying out specific stretching exercises. For these the back should be straight and the back muscles relaxed in order to prevent the vertebrae bending forward thus placing greater pressure on the discs. (Diag. 66-67) When the back muscles are not relaxed and the vertebrae bent forwards, the sciatic nerve also comes under too great a pressure.

Diag. 66: Correct!   Diag. 67: Wrong!

9.4 The Adductor Muscles

9.4.1 Terms and biomechanics

The three adductor muscles link the pelvic girdle and the pubic bone with the femur (thigh bone) and control the movement of the leg. (Diag. 68)

If the adductors are shortened the leg has a lesser range of extension. A shortening on one side is often due to a leg length discrepancy (s. chpt. III, 2.1) and occurs on the side of the shorter leg, giving an asymmetrical movement when running.

Diag. 68:

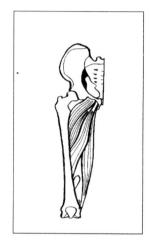

9.4.2 Diagnosis

When lying flat on the back with the leg muscles slackened, the leg on the side of the shortened muscle has a lesser range of movement.

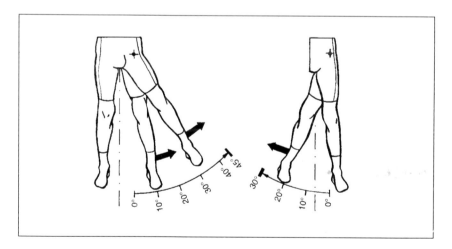

Diag. 69:
The normal comparative figures for range of movement of the hip joint. Pulling up 30-45 degrees, pushing inwards 20-30 degrees.

9.4.3   Procedures

Directed stretching exercises with muscles well warmed-up. (see Diags. 70-72)

Diags. 70-72:
Through directed stretching exercises the range of movement of the leg can be improved. In the case of a shorter leg on the same side an orthopaedic or sports doctor should be consulted to compare leg lengths. For stretching exercises on the one side, the other leg should be bent to minimize the vertical tilting of the pelvis and sideward bending of the vertebrae.

9.5   The Calf Muscle and Achilles' Tendon

9.5.1   Terms and Biomechanics

The calf muscle not only controls the strong stretching of the foot, but also supports the bending of the knee at the same time. When running it passes the force needed to lift the body in the take-off phase through the Achilles' tendon and the inside of the heel bone. (Diag. 73)
The shortening of the calf muscle causes increased tension in the Achilles' tendon during the last part of the rolling and the take-off phase of running. (Diag. 73) Hence the take-off phase is shortened and less force is exerted.
With a more pronounced shortening of the muscle (pointed foot) heel running becomes impossible. Most athletes then become frontfoot runners and are more disposed to overuse problems.

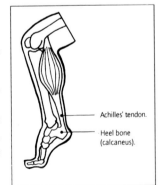

Achilles' tendon.

Heel bone (calcaneus).

Diag. 73

9.5.2 Diagnosis

Normally the upper ankle joint can actively (through its own strength) or passively (through external pressure) be pulled up 10-20 degrees further than the right angle created with the lower leg. (Diag. 74)

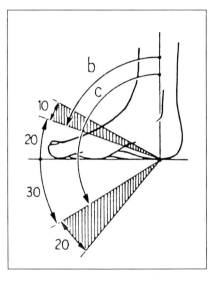

Diag. 74:
Normal range of movement for the upper ankle joint:
unshaded = active range of movement.
shaded = passive range achieved through externally pushing down.

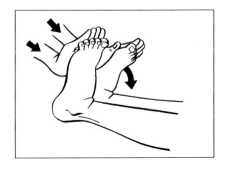

Diag. 75:
By pushing the foot upwards one can tell whether there is a difference in the movement of the ankle joints, and whether the Achilles' tendon on the side of the shorter muscle comes under greater pressure than that of the other leg at the same angle.

9.5.3 Procedures

Diag. 76:
Stretching exercises for well warmed-up muscles.
Diag. 77:
By regularly doing the stretching exercises for the calf muscles, the shortening of the muscle can be overcome more easily and problems prevented. Be careful! Where limited movement is caused by joint problems can be exacerbated.

Diag. 76   Diag. 77

9.6 Front Muscles of the Lower Leg

9.6.1 Terms and Biomechanics

The front muscle of the lower leg attaches broadly to the front side of the head of the tibia (shin bone) and continues downwards into a long tendon, reaching as far as the base of the first of the metatarsal. (Diag. 78) It controls the lifting and supination position of the foot. If this muscle shortens the range of mobility of the foot is limited and oversupination results.

Both of these limitations have serious effects for the runner. The limited mobility of the foot shortens the take-off phase. The supination position causes the pressure to be placed wrongly on the foot, and a rolling over the outside of the sole of the foot to occur. The runner is then prone to injury, especially when running on slightly sloping surfaces (street cambers). (Diag. 79)

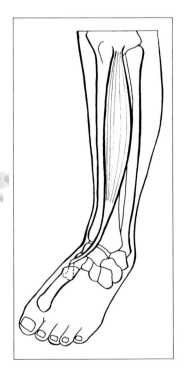

Diag. 78

Diag. 79:
With a left sloping camber the lower ankle joint of the right leg is forced into a pronation position. The increased strain of the tendons of M. tibialis anterior can lead to overuse of the muscles and tendons (tibialis anterior or front compartment syndrome). On a right sloping camber the supination of the right foot means a danger of spraining and injuring the outer ankle ligaments.

9.6.2 Diagnosis

The shortened muscles mean that the lowering of the foot into a supination position is limited. A treadmill analysis enables easy diagnosis of this condition. (s. chpt. V, 2.2.2)

9.6.3 Procedures

Correct choice of shoes, namely from sports orthopaedic specialists. Directed exercises for the muscles which straighten the foot can help preventatively or as treatment. (Diag. 80)

Diag. 80:
With well-warmed muscles specific stretching exercises lead to improved flexibility in the feet.

9.7   Fibula Muscles

9.7.1   *Terms and Biomechanics*

Both calf muscles are broadly attached along the tibia. Both tendons run behind the outer fibula bone. While the short tendon of the calf muscles reaches to the base of the fifth metatarsal, the long tendon stretches further along the sole of the foot as far as the base of the first metatarsal.

Both muscles control the pronation of the foot while also supporting the foot as it stretches out. (Diag. 81)

In the case of shortened calf muscles the foot is held in a pronation position and the normal supination movement of the foot is limited. For the runner this hyperpronation places a strain on the lower ankle joint during the landing and take-off phases. This overuse can lead to outer compartment syndrome (s. chpt. IV, 8).

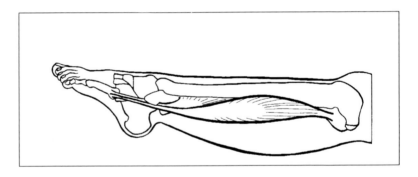

Diag. 81:
How the calf muscle looks and works.

9.7.2   *Diagnosis*

Supination of the outstretched foot is limited and the calf muscle tendons are placed under an increased strain under a greater strain than that placed on the other leg in the same position.

9.7.3   Procedures

The correct choice of shoes or, even better, shoes specially adapted by an orthopaedic specialist should be ensured (s. chpt. V, 2). Stretching exercises, such as those in 9.6.3, pull the feet inwards when maximally stretched, placing them in a supination position. (Diag. 82)

Diag. 82:
Stretching exercises which should only be carried out on well-warmed muscles.

10.   Muscular Imbalances and Strength Deficiencies

10.1   Terms and Biomechanics

The best style of running occurs when both sides of the body are equal, giving ergonomically balanced movement. Asymmetrical motion is linked to unnecessary additional movement and can have performance limiting effects. This additional movement is mostly due to the compensatory balancing efforts of shortened or weakened muscles. The runner should not accept this weak point, he should endeavour to discover the cause of the problem and the eventual muscle deficits, strengthen the weakened muscles and bring about symmetrical running movements. Asymmetrical motion with compensatory movement not only costs strength and energy, but is also a latent cause of a multitude of overuse problems.

10.2   Diagnosis

As an example; well-developed gluteal muscles are important for the equilibrium of the whole body. Underdeveloped, or one-sided, gluteal muscles mean that the neighbouring trunk and leg muscles have to work harder to stabilise and balance the body, thus giving rise to asymmetrical movement of the body. Some simple tests (Diag. 83), or test exercises, (Diag. 84) can help to uncover these deficits.

Diag. 83:
The Trendelenburg Test checks the
strength of the gluteal muscles
(M. glutaeus medius). Strong gluteal
muscles are necessary to stabilise
the pelvis and vertebrae when
standing on one leg (a).
If the muscles are weak the pelvis
tilts horizontally and the vertebrae
bend sidewards. One side of the
pelvis then stands higher than the
other (b).

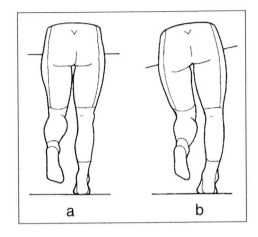

10.3   Test Exercises to Discover Muscular Deficiencies

Many runners suffer from one-sided deficiencies in the strength of the muscles or deficiencies in specific areas. The following test exercises (from **Spring, Kunz, Schneider, Tritschler** and **Unold**) help to highlight these problems. The same exercises can also serve to strengthen the muscles. The exercises should be repeated, and counted in two second phases, until fatigue sets in.

The number of repeats carried out, as recorded in the table, corresponds to the degree of weakness, taking into account the age-group.

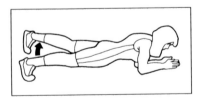

Diag. 84:
*The **trunk muscles** test relies on using*
the arms to support the body.
Alternatively raise each leg a foot
eight from the floor in second bursts.

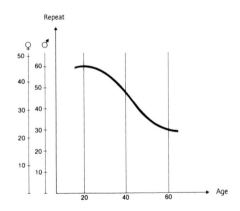

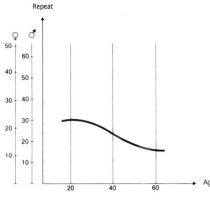

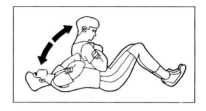

Diag. 85:
Lying on the back, with the arms crossed over the chest and legs bent, tests the **stomach muscles**: lift the upper body and roll forwards.

Diag. 86:
Lifting the trunk upright, keeping the back straight, whilst kneeling with the arms crossed, tests the **back muscles**.

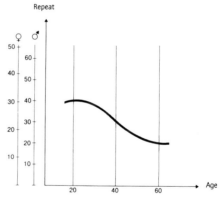

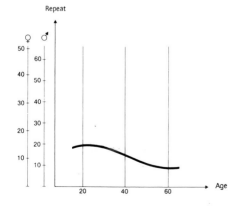

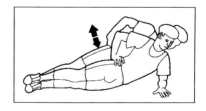

Diag. 87:
To test the **side trunk muscles** lie on the side, using the elbows to support the pelvis as you raise the pelvis until the trunk is straight.

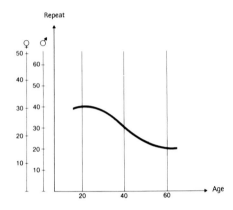

Diag. 88:
*Lie on the side with the lower leg bent and raise the upper leg in two second efforts. This tests the outer **hip flexor muscles**.*
Repeat on the other side.

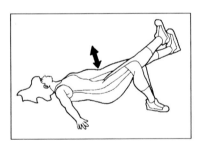

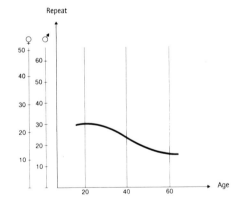

Diag. 89:
*Lying on the back with one leg supporting, and the other outstretched, enables the **rear hamstring and hip muscles** to be tested. The pelvis should be pushed upwards until the trunk is straight. Change legs in two second efforts.*

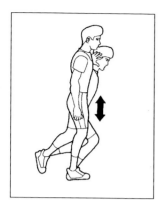
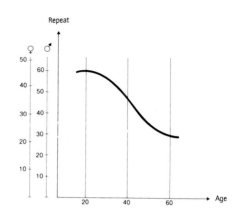

Diag. 90:
The **thigh muscles** can be tested by standing on one leg and bending the leg to an angle of 60 degrees, then straightening again in two second efforts. Keep balance by supporting yourself.

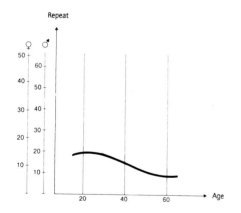
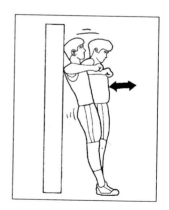

Diag. 91:
In order to test and train the **shoulder blade stabilisers**, stand sloping back on to a wall (1 1/2 foot lengths out from the wall) and, with elbows bent, push the body in two second efforts 3 cm out from the wall. Do not allow the shoulder blades to touch the wall.

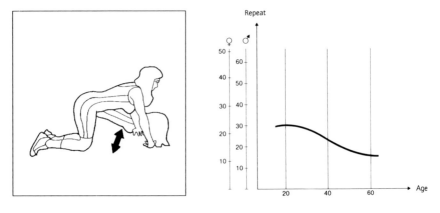

Diag. 92:
*Stand on all fours and bend both elbows in two second efforts without changing the position of the legs and pelvis. This checks the rear **upper arm muscles**.*

Diagrams 84-92 taken from:
Spring/Kunz/Schneider/Tritschler/Unold: "Kraft – Theorie und Praxis", Georg Thieme Verlag, Stuttgart 1990, p. 31-47

10.4   Procedures

The test exercises also work as training exercises to strengthen affected muscles or areas of the body. Additionally strength training is recommended. Physiotherapy is only necessary in the case of pronounced imbalances or deformities.

IV   Most Common Overuse Problems with a Check List for Self-diagnosis

Overburdening the body through forced or inadequate training, bad choice of ground, or wearing ill-fitting shoes, particularly where biological factors limiting performance were already in play, can give rise to the first sign of overburdening the foot, lower leg, knee or vertebrae. Most often it is a case of overstraining the tendons, tendon attachments, tendon sheaths or the muscles. The first signs of a strain do not need to be treated as an injury, they clear up without medical help when the cause is corrected.

If this does not occur the consequences are overuse injuries and even irreparable damage to the health of the athlete.

Therefore the recognition of performance limiting biological characteristics and of the first signs of overuse are very important.

The best preventative measure is self-analysis which involves checking for the most frequent causes of overuse problems. In this way the runner can react swiftly and correctly and avoid the need to seek professional treatment for overuse injuries later.

To help with this we have listed below the most frequent overuse problems in running, namely those associated with the foot, the lower leg, the knee joint, the pelvis and the vertebrae:

1.   Lower Back and Pelvic Problems (Lumbago)

1.1   Signs (Symptoms)

Increased pain in the lower back during or after running.

1.2   Biological Changes

The overburdening and irritation of the discs, the vertebrae supports and even the small joints of the vertebrae themselves cause the pain. (hollow back, s. chpt. III, 1)

1.3   Check List of Causes

• Insufficient warming-up of the back muscles and lack of adequate stretching before running.
• Insufficient stretching exercises for the back muscles after running.
• Running on hard surfaces (road running).
• Running on mountainous and undulating terrain (s. chpt. II, 3).
• Insufficient strength in the back, trunk and stomach muscles (often due to a sedentary occupation).
• Muscular imbalances (leg length discrepancies, s. chpt. III, 10).
• Incorrect training shoes or insufficient shock absorption.

1.4   Procedures

Establish the causes of the problems through thorough investigation. Discover and overcome individual performance limiting characteristics. (s. chpt. III) Check training shoes. Back exercises to strengthen the back and stomach muscles (see recommended exercises). With ongoing or recurring lower back problems consult a doctor.

Recommended Exercises to Strengthen the Back Muscles (from Bürkle)
Ten Minute Programme. Repeat each Exercise 2-3 Times

Diag. 93:
Purpose of exercise:
Stretch and strengthen the vertebrae and trunk muscles through systematic exercises.

Method:
Kneeling on all fours pull the stomach in and the head towards the chest. The back is pulled upwards into a cat stretch and the head is pulled backwards. Then gently push the vertebrae downwards. To make it more difficult the posterior can be pushed towards the heels while the back is held in the cat stretch position.

Diag. 94:
Purpose of exercise:
Strengthen posterior and back muscles and work on balance.

Method:
Support yourself on your hands and knees with elbows slightly bent, hold the back straight by tensing the stomach and posterior muscles. Alternately straighten one leg out behind, pulling the toes in and pushing the head forwards. By stretching one leg and the opposite arm at the same time the exercise can be made more difficult.

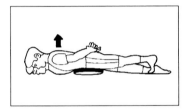

Diag. 95:
Purpose of exercise:
Stabilise the back muscles by tensing the body and stretching.

Method:
Lie with the forehead on the floor and hands on the backside, tense the posterior and stomach muscles, push the heels backwards and lift the head slightly. In order to avoid a hollow back, place a firm cushion or pillow under the stomach for support.

To achieve a greater degree of difficulty raise the hands and hold high for a short time.

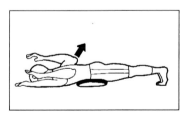

Diag. 96:
Purpose of the exercise:
Strengthen the back and chest muscles.

Method:
Lie on the stomach with the arms next to the head in a U-position. Build up a base tension and raise both arms pushing the shoulder blades together (in the direction of the vertebrae).
Extra difficulty:
Make swimming movements with the arms.

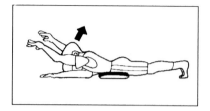

Diag. 97:
Purpose of exercise:
Strengthen back muscles.

Method:
Lie on the stomach arms flat on the floor and slightly bent, slightly raise the arms and upper body and slowly bend to the left and right, without forming a hollow back.

Diag. 98:
Purpose of exercise:
Stretching of hamstring muscles.

Method:
Sit with the upper body straight and knees pushed down straight. Feet at right angles, head stretched upwards.
Difficulty: Lift the arms up and slowly turn the trunk left and right, this strengthens the trunk and mobilizes the vertebrae.

Exercises to Strengthen the Back Muscles for Sit-down Jobs (Do exercises for 1-2 minutes every 30 minutes)

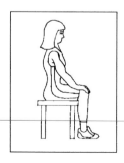

The following sitting exercises, originally designed to help people with sedentary jobs strengthen back muscles (from Bürkle), nevertheless are useful for runners as they strengthen and stabilise the muscles of the neck, back, chest and lower back.

Diag. 99:
Purpose of exercise:
Straighten the vertebrae, correct breathing technique.

Method:
Sitting in an upright position, swing gently to and fro from a rounded back to a hollow back position. Whilst the gluteal and stomach muscles are tensed, and the shoulder blades pushed back and down, you should gently breathe out.

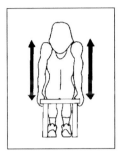

Diag. 100:
Purpose of exercise:
Strengthen the shoulders and neck muscles.

Method:
Sit with the feet shoulder width apart and the back upright. You should tense the stomach and gluteal muscles while pressing the feet downwards. Push the shoulders down and pull the head upwards thus stretching the vertebrae. Alternately raise the shoulders upwards, hold the tension, and then push down again.

Finally cross the shoulders forwards and backwards. Keep the head relaxed.

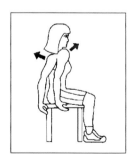

Diag. 101:
Purpose of exercise:
Stretch and strengthen the chest and shoulder muscles.

Method:
After you have built a basic sitting tension, push the shoulders down and backwards (push the shoulder blades together). Then, whilst the shoulders are pushed forwards towards the nose, ensure that the head is pulled upwards and the stomach and gluteal muscles remain taut.

Diag. 102:
Purpose of exercise:
Strengthen and mobilise shoulder and neck
muscles.

Method:
Sit with the thumbs in the armpit and circle the bent arms forwards and backwards.
The shoulders control a large circular movement.

Diag. 103:
Purpose of exercise:
Stabilise the vertebrae of the neck and strengthen the
neck muscles.

Method:
Sit with the hands linked behind the head and use the hands to exert and release
pressure. Do not press so hard that the exercise
becomes uncomfortable.

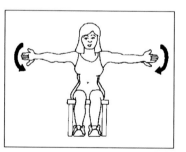

Diag. 104:
Purpose of exercise:
Mobilise the shoulders, stabilise neck and
shoulder muscles.

Method:
Sit with arms stretched out sidewards and turn the outstretched arms as far as
possible forwards and backwards. By allowing the arms to circle forwards and
backwards this exercise can be varied and extended.

Exercises to Strengthen the Stomach and Trunk Muscles. Ten Minute Programme. Repeat each Exercise 10-20 Times

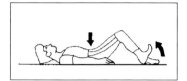

Diag. 105:
Purpose of exercise:
To test the tension of the stomach muscles and the mobility of the vertebrae.

Method:
Lie on the back with knees bent and feet together and raise the tip of your foot towards you, keeping the heels on the floor. Tense the stomach and gluteal muscles thus pressing the vertebrae onto the floor.

Diag. 106:
Purpose of exercise:
Strengthen trunk muscles and body tension.

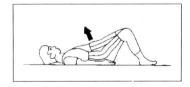

Method:
Lie on the back with legs slightly bent and feet flat on the floor. Slowly lift the hips straightening the spine (see diagram).

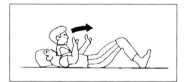

Diag. 107:
Purpose of exercise:
Train the straight stomach muscles.

Method:
Lie on the back and build up a basic tension, lift the head and shoulders slightly. Push bent arms against an imaginary resistance. When you can, push both hands against the thighs the exercise needs to be made more difficult.

Diag. 108:
Purpose of exercise:
Strengthening of the sloping stomach muscles.

Method:
Lift upright from lying down pushing, for example, the right knee with the left hand, hold the tension 5-10 seconds. Repeat for the other side.

Diag. 109:
Purpose of exercise:
Strengthen various muscle groups from the shoulder blades to the calves (including amongst others the sloping stomach muscles).

Method:
Pull up from lying down pushing against the floor with the left leg and the right arm. The right leg should be bent and the left hand pushed against the knee. Alternate sides.

Diag. 110:
Purpose of exercise:
Strengthen and stretch thigh, gluteal and trunk muscles.

Method:
Lie down and grip the right knee with both hands, pulling it to the chest. Push the stretched arms against the resistance of the hands, alternate sides. To make it more difficult pull both legs in pushing the head between the knees.

Diag. 111:
Purpose of exercise:
Become aware of muscles tensing and relaxing.

Method:
Lie down with the legs forming a right angle against a wall, push lightly with the feet and press the vertebrae against the floor. Slowly build up tension and relax.

2.   Chafing Syndrome in the Knee Joint

2.1   Symptoms

Pain on the outside of the upper knee joint when bending and stretching the knee, at its worst when the knee is bent at a 30 degree angle. Increase in pain with increased loading. (Diag. 113)

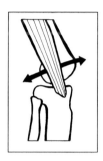

Diag. 112:
Grating position of
the tendon of the
ilio tibialis tractus.

Diag. 113:
Pain zone.

2.2   Biological Changes

Aggravation of the bursa through the rubbing of the ilio tibialis tractus over the cupola of the outer thighbone roller with inflammation of the underlying bursas. (Diag. 112)

2.3   Check List of Causes

• Long training runs, e.g. preparing for a marathon running on hard ground.
• Hill and mountain running.
• Forced weight training.
• Insufficient warm-up and stretching before running.
• Propensity of the runner towards O-legs or hyperpronation problems.
• Inadequate or worn out shoes.

2.4   Measures

Ice packs, resting for several days, eventual cross-training to maintain fitness. When restarting training avoid hill running. No weight training for several weeks. Check shoes. If problem continues consult a sports doctor.

3. Aggravation of the Knee Groove Muscles (Popliteus Tendonitus)

3.1   Symptoms

Coincidental experience of pain while putting pressure on the outside of the knee joint, getting stronger with a bent or turned out knee. Eventual spreading of the pain into the knee groove, worsening in cross-legged position or when legs are crossed over on top of each other. (Diag. 114-115)

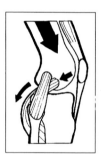

Diag. 114:
Starting position of
M. popliteus.

Diag. 115:
Pain point on the
outer side of the
knee joint (outer
thighbone roller).

3.2   Biological changes

The popliteus muscle bends and turns the knee inwards. If the knee is turned and loaded too strongly outwards an irritation arises on the attachment of the muscle to the thigh bone roller of the kneecap aggravating the underlying bursa.

3.3   Check List of Causes

- Running up and down hills, hill-reps.
- Running on soft ground, cross-country, "tartan" tracks.
- Propensity of runner towards hyperpronation of the feet.
- Inadequate shoes.

3.4   Measures

Ice packs, break from training for a few days, when restarting avoid hills and heavy weight training. Check shoes for inadequate support of the inner foot edge. If pain continues consult a sports doctor.

4. Patella Pain (Chondropathia Patellae)

4.1 Symptoms

Pain originating from the kneecap area, worsened when the knee is loaded or bent, especially when going up or downstairs. (Diag. 116) When the kneecap pushes sideways pressure on it hurts. (Diag. 117)

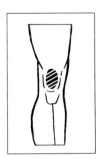

Diag. 116:
Area of pain

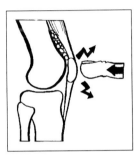

Diag. 117:
Pain when pressure is exerted on the kneecap.

4.2 Biological Changes

Irritation of the joint between the kneecap and the sliding groove on the thigh bone through increased pressure of the kneecap on the thigh bone when the thigh muscles are tensed.

4.3 Check List of Causes

- Too long training runs, e.g. when preparing for a marathon.
- Mountain or hill running, long training runs on hard ground.
- Propensity of runner towards X-legs.
- Inadequate shoes.
- Insufficient warm-up and muscle stretching before running.
- Overweight runner.

4.4 Measures

Hot and cold treatment, stretching of the thigh muscles, avoid bending the knee for long periods, training break for several days, eventual cross-training to maintain fitness. Check shoes, reduce weight. If problems continue consult a sports doctor.

5.   Roughened Patella Syndrome (Jumper's Knee)

5.1   Symptoms

Overloading pain on the lower part of the kneecap and the length of the patella tendon, especially when the knee joint is bent and load-bearing. Sensitivity to pressure and pain in the lower part of the kneecap and the upper part of the patella tendon. (Diag. 118)

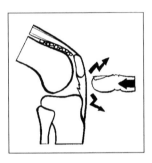

Diag. 118:
Sensitivity to pressure
on the lower edge of
the kneecap, at the
point of fraying of
the patella tendon.

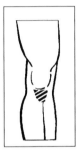

Diag. 119:
Point of pain
under the
kneecap.

5.2   Biological Changes

Irritation of the attachment of the patella tendon onto the kneecap, fraying fibrous tissue changes of the patella tendon on the underside of the kneecap.

5.3   Check List of Causes

• Intensive jump loading from a combination of running and jumping training.
• Too intensive weight training with hypertrophy of the quadriceps muscle.
• Shortening of the ischiocrurale muscles.
• Inherent raising of the kneecap.
• Forced mountain or hill training.

5.4   Measures

Ice packs, training break from a few days up to a few weeks, eventual cross-training to maintain fitness, avoid bending the knee, wear a knee bandage whenever putting pressure on the knee. Check shoes, if problems continue consult a sports doctor.

6. Shin Splints

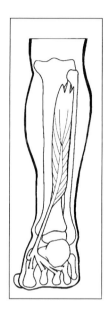

Diag. 120:
Rear attachment point of M. tibialis posterior

Diag. 121:
Area of pain

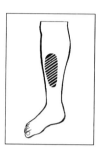

6.1 Symptoms

Pain and sensitivity to pressure along the length of the inner front edge of the shin bone, worse at the end of a training run.

6.2 Biological Changes

Irritation of the surface of the bone at the attachment of M. tibialis posterior onto the back of the shin and calf with reflexive projection of the pain onto the front inside of the lower leg.

6.3 Check List of causes

- Little or no warm-up and stretching before running.
- Overlong training runs.
- Sinking of the foot arch with hyperpronation due to overtired muscles.
- Dropped arches.
- Running on sloping surfaces (cambers).
- Running on hard surfaces (too much road running).
- Cross-country running, especially on muddy ground.
- Unaccustomed running on "tartan" tracks, especially in spikes.
- Inadequate or worn out shoes.
- Inexperienced runner or a beginner.

6.4 Measures

Ice packs, training break for several days, cross-training to maintain fitness or limiting of training, check shoes, maybe orthosis, treadmill analysis. With ongoing problems consult a sports doctor.

7. Front Compartment Syndrome

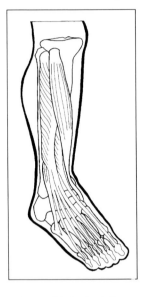

Diag. 122:
Course of the front swollen lower leg muscles

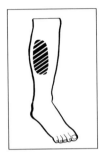

Diag. 123:
Area of pain

7.1 Symptoms

Palm-sized painful and sensitive area in the middle to upper section of the front and side lower leg. Occasional strange sensations on the stretched side of the inter digital fan between the big and second toes. (Diag. 122)

7.2 Biological Changes

Swelling of the overloaded front shin muscles with increased pressure developing in the front muscle compartment, occasionally also causing compression of the peronaeus profundus nerve.

7.3 Check List of Causes

- Little or no warm-up and stretching before running.
- Speed training on very soft ground.
- Barefoot running on the beach.
- Use of spikes when track ("tartan") training or cross-country running.
- Hill running.
- Unaccustomed change from flat to hill running on soft ground.

7.4 Measures

Icing the front of the leg. Training break for several days. Avoidance of possible causes. Check shoes before resuming training. Cross-training to maintain fitness. With ongoing problems consult a sports doctor.

8.   Outer Compartment Syndrome

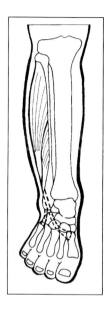

Diag. 124:
Course of the swollen
calf muscle

Diag. 125:
Area of pain

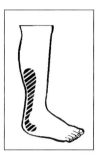

8.1 Symptoms

The back of the leg is painful and sensitive to touch on the outer bone and the lower part of the calf with eventual swelling.

8.2   Biological Changes

Swelling of the calf muscle (M. peronaeus longus and brevis) with occasional irritation of the tendon sheathes in the joint region behind and on the outer bone.

8.3   Check List of Causes

• Little or no warm-up and stretching before running.
• Hyperpronation of the feet through inherent structural deficiencies.
• Long training runs on sloping surfaces (cambers).
• Barefoot running on soft ground.
• Unsuitable or worn out running shoes.

8.4   Measures

Hot and cold treatment, training break for a few days, cross-training to maintain fitness, ankle support, check shoes. With persistent problems consult a sports doctor.

9.   Inflammation of the Tendon Sheathes in the Foot

9.1   Symptoms

Pain, swelling and sensitivity to pressure on the front of the foot, which gets worse as the athlete flexes the foot.

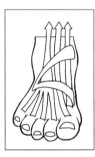

Diag. 126:
Anatomy of the foot levers

Diag. 127:
Painful area of the ankle

9.2   Biological Changes

Inflammation and bruising of the tendon sheathes arises from the overuse of the straight tendons of the musculus extensor digitorum longus and extensor hallucis longus, which pass, shrouded in tendon sheathes, under the front, width ways, ligaments of the foot.

9.3   Check List of Causes

- Little or no warm-up and stretching before running.
- Heavy speed training on soft surfaces.
- Barefoot running on the beach.
- Use of spikes during track, "tartan" running or cross-country running.
- Hill running.
- Incorrect shoes.

9.4   Measures

Hot and cold treatment, break from training for several days. When resuming training avoid all above causes. Check shoes. If problems persist consult a sports doctor.

10. Irritation of the Achilles' Tendon (Achilles tendonitus)

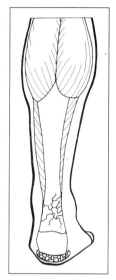

10.1   Symptoms

Pain, resulting in sensitivity to touch and swelling of the Achilles' tendon, particularly during the push off phase of running. Experience of pain when standing on tiptoe on one leg.

10.2   Biological Changes

Irritation and swelling of the tissue along the path of the Achilles' tendon.

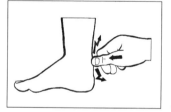

Diag. 128

10.3   Checklist of Causes

Diag. 129

- Little or no warm-up and stretching before running.
- Overloading and misuse of the Achilles' tendon due to imbalances caused by the problem.
- Other causes, e.g. hyperpronation, blisters, chafing.
- Running with feet splayed out.
- Alternation between heel and forefoot running (track training in spikes).
- Hill running.
- Barefoot running on soft ground (beach running).
- Overemphasis in the take-off phase during technical training.
- Inadequate shoes.
- Overweight runner.

10.4   Measures

Ice packs, heel raises or supports to relieve the Achilles' tendon, training break for a few days up to a few weeks. Weight reduction. Alternative cross-training to maintain fitness. If the swelling does not dissipate, despite momentary disappearance of pain, there is a danger of re-occurrence; ultimately sports orthosis, treadmill analysis. If problems still persist consult a sports doctor.

11. Inflammation of the Achilles' Tendon Bursa

11.1   Symptoms

Pain, sensitivity to touch and painful swelling behind the Achilles' tendon at the lower attachment of the tendon to the heel bone. (Diag. 130)

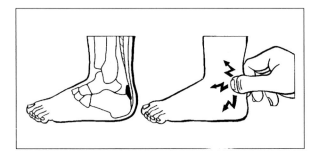

Diag. 130:
Area of the pain and sensitivity in the case of inflammation of the Achilles' bursa

11.2   Biological Changes

Located in the angle between the Achilles' tendon and heel bone the bursa can swell due to too severe chafing and loading. This can be worsened through inherent upper heel spurs – Haglund heel.

11.3   Check List of Causes

• As with Achilles' tendon inflammation, see point 10.
• Running on the balls of the feet.
• Hill running.
• Stressing and badly loading the Achilles' tendon through compensation due to other problems such as (build up of blisters, hyperpronation due to tiredness, chafing).
• Haglund heel.
• Overweight.

11.4   Measures

As with inflammation of the Achilles' tendon.

12. Ganglion of the Achilles' Tendon (Heel Knots)

12.1   Symptoms

A shiny coloured lump occurs on the heel bone on the outside of the lower attachment of the Achilles' tendon to the heel bone. Tends to chafing and Achilles' tendon problems.

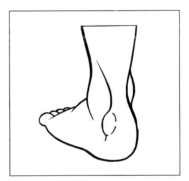

Diag. 131:
Typical build up of a
knot on the Achilles'
tendon

12.2   Biological Changes

Large, firm lump on the outside of the Achilles' tendon attachment to the heel. (Diag. 131)

12.3   Measures

Running shoes to fit with cushioned heel cup to avoid chafing.

13. Heel Spur Syndrome

13.1   Symptoms

Problems and pain in the area of the heel bone when putting pressure on the sole of the foot.

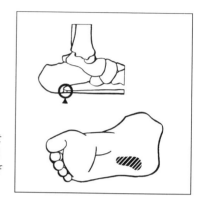

Diag. 132:
The typical pain during use is not caused by the bony point (heel spur) but rather through the inflammation of the plantar fascia.

13.2   Biological Changes

Irritation of the attachment of the plantar fascia onto the heel bone, occasionally in conjunction with a bony growth on the heel bone (heel spur).

13.3   Checklist of Causes

• Faulty stance, running on too hard ground (road running).
• Hill training.
• Common in runners with hollow foot problems or tendencies towards hyperpronation.
• Inadequate or worn out shoes.
• Overweight.

13.4   Measures

Several weeks break from training, maintain fitness by cross-training, soft inserts, padding at the point of pain. Build up feet muscles (gripping exercises for the toes). Correct choice of shoes with good heel stability, and a shock absorption system which corresponds to body weight.
    Commissioning of special shoes/orthosis[1] from an orthopaedic shoemaker (sport orthosis to protect the plantar fascia).

---

[1] Orthopaedic device with posture-correcting and supporting function.

14. Big Toe Problems

14.1 Symptoms

Pain in the joint at the base of the big toe, particularly in the roll through and take-off phases of running or after training.

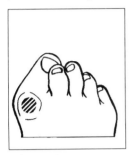

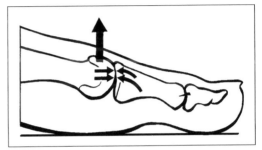

Diag. 133:
Hallux valgus

Diag. 134:
Cause of pain in the case of hallux limitus or
rigidus

14.2 Biological Changes

Deformation of the big toe as with a crooked toe or through shortened tendons (hallux limitus) or changes in the joint (hallux rigidus) together with a limited flexibility of the base joint of the big toe. Tendency to build up calluses. Pain due to the misloading of the big toe through a crooked toe (overuse problems in the case of a stiff toe in the area of the joint).

14.3 Check List of Causes

• Toe deformities (hallux valgus).
• Limited flexibility of the big toe (hallux rigidus, hallux limitus).
• Hill running.
• Barefoot sand running.

14.4 Measures

Self-evaluation of the degree of performance limiting changes. Specific suitable shoes, alter training and running programme to suit. If you experience pain when standing consult a specialist doctor.

15. Pressure Points and Calluses on the Soles of the Feet and Toes (Corns)

15.1   Symptoms

Hard skin and the build-up of calluses can lead to an inflamed and painful reaction.

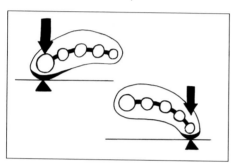

Diag. 135:
In the case of pronation and faulty loading of the foot the pressure points and calluses occur mostly on the inner region of the ball of the foot, with supination they occur on the outer edge of the sole.

15.2 Biological Changes

The build-up of calluses occurs on the outside at the points stressed by deformities or the wrong loading of the foot and toes.

15.3   Check List of Causes

* Badly fitting shoes (too small or too narrow) with poor or insufficient absorption in the ball of the foot.
* Feet deformities (s. chpt. III).
* Running without socks.
* Barefoot running.
* Long runs on the road.

15.4   Measures

Appropiate running shoes in the case of feet deformities, adaptation of shoes by specialist orthopaedic shoemakers, consult a specialist doctor for correction of serious deformities.

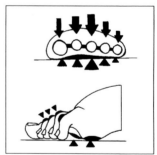

Diag. 136:
In the case of a dropped arch the mid area of the ball of the foot takes the pressure. With hammer toe the tops of the toe joints rub on the shoe and the ball of the foot takes a great deal of pressure on the underside.

16. Blood under the Toenails

16.1   Symptoms

Dark blue colouring of the toenails with painful swelling of the nail beds.

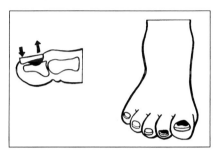

Diag. 137 a:
Pressure on the edge of the nail lifts the nail from the nail bed, a painful blood blister develops under the nail giving it dark colouring.

16.2   Biological Changes

Repeated pressure on the end of the nail causes it to lift out of the nail bed tearing the small blood vessel causing bleeding under the nail. The raising of the nail and nail bed causes the pain.

16.3   Check List of Causes

- Too small and too narrow running shoes.
- Toenails too long.
- Nail deformities (fungus infections).
- Toe deformities.

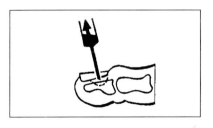

16.4   Measures

Proper fitting shoes. Chiropodist nail care. With existing painful blood blisters consult a doctor. Medically trained runners can relieve the blood pressure by puncturing the nail themselves under sterile condition. Be careful! Unsterilised work can lead to infection.

Diag. 137 b:
After disinfecting the nail and the nail bed a sterile syringe is used to perforate the nail and draw the blood out, relieving the nail. Afterwards sterile dressings should be used for 48 hours.

17. Meniscus Troubles

17.1   Symptoms

Sudden or lingering pain on the outside or inside of the knee joint, in particular when twisting the body while standing still, can be the first sign of an injury or wear and tear of the menisci (outer or inner).

17.2   Biological Changes

The menisci are half-moon shaped cartilaginous discs in the knee joint that balance out the strong curve of the thigh bone roller as it passes over the flat surface of the joint, with the shin bone enabling a turning movement of the knee joint (see Diag. 138 a). Through use small tears occur in the meniscus, causing pain in the affected part of knee joint. Tears can be shallow, but also lead to a complete tear of the whole meniscus with immediate blocking of movement.

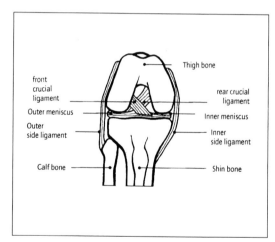

Diag. 138 a:
The outer and inner menisci are cartilaginous discs lying between the surfaces of the joints that enable the rotational movement of the knee joint.

17.3   Check List of Causes

- O-leg deformity is particular responsible for premature wear on the inner meniscus.
- Sudden twisting of the knee joint on uneven ground.
- Overweight.

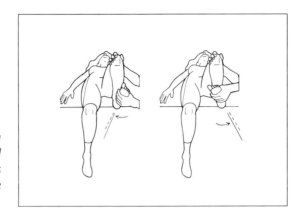

Diag. 138 b:
Pain manifests itself when bending the knee and turning the foot inwards and outwards on the side of the damaged meniscus.

17.4 Measures

Several days break form training. With painful blocked movement, repeated pain and varied intense pain over several weeks, seek the advice of a G.P., Sport or Orthopaedic doctor.

18. Alternative Sports Training to Maintain Fitness during Overuse Injuries

In every type of endurance sport and distance running attention should be paid to four types of training:

1. Training of the movement and support apparatus of the body (muscles and joints).
2. Training for the heart and circulation.
3. Training for the metabolism (energy release through fat burning).
4. Psychological training (dedication, endurance and preparation, ability to overcome difficulties in order to train harder).

The whole spectrum of training does not need to break down just because of the collapse or irritation of one part of the body. There are many possibilities to keep up fitness and condition. The idea of continuing to train every other part of the body should be kept in mind, while resting and sparing only the affected muscles or tendons. There are many other alternative training programmes which serve this purpose. The following table lists a few of the alternative sports with relevance to running.

Alternative sports programmes to maintain all-round endurance and strength

In the case of overuse injuries we recommend all types of sports which work the upper body and upper extremities.

Overuse problem:	Alternative sport:			
	Cycling	Cross-country skiing in winter/roller-skiing in summer	Weight training	Aqua-jogging
1. Small of the back and pelvis	—	**	*	**
2. Chafing syndrome of the knee	*	—	—	*
3. Popliteus tendon tendonitis	*	—	**	*
4. Chondropathia patella (no quadriceps)	—	**	*	*
5. Spiky Patella Syndrome (no quadriceps)	—	**	*	*
6. Front Compartment Syndrome	*	*	**	*
7. Shin Splints	**	**	**	*
8. Outer Compartment Syndrome	*	*		*
9. Achilles' tendonitis (not of the calf)	—	—	*	*
10. Inflamed Achilles' tendon bursa	—	—	—	*
11. Inflamed tendon sheathes in the feet	—	—	**	*
12. Heel spur (plantarfascitis)	**	*	**	**
13. Hallux valgus and limitus	**	*	**	**

Symbols: — not suitable   * suitable with certain condition   ** suitable

V   Steps towards Optimising Performance

1.   Standard Running Shoes

1.1   Purpose

Runners, and especially distance runners, need specially designed running shoes. These need to be able to absorb the impact of body weight during the landing phase, give the foot sufficient lateral support in the standing phase, and fully support and guide it in the rolling and take-off phases. Finally they must steer and direct the body's momentum correctly.

1.1.1   Absorption

Shock absorption is of fundamental importance during the landing phase of running. As speed increases so too does the power which passes through the foot, as the body strikes the ground. The heel must absorb up to five times the body weight and dissipate the shock from striking the ground.

We know from detailed studies that, during running, the forces at work act in less than a third of a second, while when walking, ground contact lasts about a second. In the running position the body weight impacts on the ground at an angle.

On hard asphalt or concrete the shoe is abruptly stopped and the shock absorption must act. On softer ground the impulse is not totally stopped, the runner continues a few millimetres into the ground. This gentler landing can be seen as an element of shock absorption.

The mid sole of the running shoe has the task of absorbing the shock. It lies between the insole and the out sole of the shoe. The structure of the absorption material is similar to that of a sponge with lots of little hollow compartments, filled with air or gas.

When subjected to pressure, these compartments become compressed and the gaseous material is able to escape. Since this always provides a delayed, holding effect, the foot meets the floor relatively evenly. The shock is therefore absorbed. As the foot lifts the material expands to regain its original size.

However, all absorption material eventually wears out and the return to the original shape is slowed down, or simply no longer happens. This can affect the whole area or just one part of it. Mid soles worn out on one side are immediately recognisable as "worn out".

For years most of the research in this field has concentrated on the absorption factor of running shoes. In 1976, the first shock absorption system was launched onto the market – a hollow chamber in the heel area of the shoe – and running shoes graduated to "high- tech" sports equipment.

Today Air-Cushion, Gel, Hydroflow, Hybrid, Trinomic, Fulcrum, Stable-Air and other running shoe systems have all entered on the scene. All have the objective of absorbing the shock effect. Some shoes also have corresponding absorption in the forefoot area.

Since the absorption systems are all built differently, so the way they work is also different. It is also obvious that according to the type of ground (hard or soft, solid or loose), and the weight of the runner, very different demands are placed on the system of absorption.

A lighter runner can get away with a shoe with softer absorption, while a heavy runner needs a strong, sturdy shoe. Were a heavy runner to wear a softer shoe, the absorption system in the mid sole would quickly wear out.

As a consequence the muscles and ligaments of the runner would begin to experience problems. On the other hand, a lighter runner will simply not be able to make proper use of the absorption system in a solid shoe and will similarly suffer irritation in his muscles and ligaments.

Many absorption systems feel too spongy at first and need a 'wearing-in' period before they lose their imprecise feeling. Additionally the layer beneath the heel cup should not be too soft, or the heel will not be adequately supported. The shoe will feel spongy and quickly becomes worn out and useless.

After several kilometres the material of the mid sole also needs time to rest. Research suggests most material used today needs around 24 hours to build itself up again. For frequent training, therefore, it is best to alternate several pairs of shoes. Constantly worn shoes wear out quicker and become unstable.

1.1.2   Support

The supporting of the foot, above all in the standing phase, is carried out by the heel cup and mid sole. The length and height of the heel cup are crucial for a stable hold, as is the strength of the sole and the stabilisers, which pass the pressure from the heel cap onto the floor. This stops the tendency of the foot to buckle under the pressures of weight and constant load.

In order to give the shoe greater stability the manufacturer must insert harder parts into the mid sole. This eliminates one-sided wear and tear, so that those tending towards pronation (clubfoot, dropped arches and splayfoot) receive the necessary support. Stabilisers in the sole and heel cup support the foot.
If the runner has a tendency to supinate, the mid sole receives no additional support on the outside edge, otherwise the foot is forced too strongly inwards.

The material used in modern shoes can no longer be compared with that of the old ones. Synthetic upper materials (i.e. Durabuck) and netting insets like Nylon have replaced yesterdays leather and canvas. Today the durability and lightness of the shoes is the most important consideration.
Often the manufacturers logo, placed in the central area between the ball of the foot and the heel, also plays a key role in the support structure. For example the famous three stripes' lacing technique gives the necessary support and also reinforces the bottom of the shoe. Textile inlays cope with the type of perspiration associated with sporting activities and improve air circulation. In the heel area the cap is strengthened with leather-type material to give the necessary stable support. Today these are made from synthetic materials.

1.1.3   Direction

We estimate that around 3/4 of the population suffer from faulty foot strike. Attention must be paid to this when choosing shoes. If the support structure of the shoe is not sufficient to bring a club-foot under control, then the shoe will only exacerbate the situation.
Unfortunately in normal sports shops the runner receives little or no advice as to which shoes suit his foot type. Problems with the Achilles' tendon, tibia, calf and knee all lead to a faulty stance which must be compensated by the shoes. Therefore it is fundamentally wrong to choose an all-round sports shoe for running. It is best to seek

the advice of an orthopaedic shoemaker/specialist in order to be able to select the most appropriate shoes. (Diag. 139 a-b)

Abb. 139 a   *Abb. 139 b*

Diags. 139 a-b:
Example of the wrong mid sole support:
a: A normal strike.
b: When the mid sole comes under pressure, the white side material made from EVA gives more than in the heel wedge. The power passes through the heel cup and through the stabilisers into the EVA, which is too soft. Since the wedge in the sole is firm the heel direction therefore becomes unstable.

1.2   Shape and Construction of the Running Shoe

Running shoes are made on a last. The lasts are decisive for the size and shape of the shoe. Women's lasts are cut narrower than men's. Some manufacturers also make shoes in two width fittings so runners can get a better fit. (Diag. 140)

Lasts are also made in different shapes according to needs. Today the lightly curved last is the most common shape, however straight lasts also have a curve of approximately six degrees. (Diag. 141)

Straight lasts are very popular with runners suffering from splayfeet or dropped arches. They also give runners who pronate the necessary foot support. Curved lasts turn inwards between the heel and the point of the foot. They accommodate runners with high arches or a tendency to supinate. When one looks at the shoe from underneath the difference is easily recognisable. When the end of the shoe points from the middle inwards (when looked at from the front), then it is a curved last. (Diag. 141)

The front part of the shoe is called the toe box. They are also made differently. Some manufacturers offer models with wider toe boxes to suit a wider foot.

The mid foot area also determines the main support of the shoe. It is the section between the heel cup and the toe box. Here the foot must be tightly and safely held in order to ensure stability and support.

Diag. 140:
Wide and narrow toe boxes

Diag. 141:
Looking at the sole of the shoe the curved last is clearly distinguishable from the straight last.

1.3   Choosing the Correct Running Shoe

We should make one point clear: the ideal running shoe for all runners does not exist. However, individual runners can find a shoe almost perfect for them, providing they choose according to individual needs and problems (body weight, running surface, feet anomalies etc.). The following criteria are of clear importance in helping the individual to choose the right shoe.

• *Foot type*
Every athlete must know his foot type: whether he has a club-foot, dropped arch, hollow foot or splayfoot, or even a combination of several types, is critical for his choice of shoe.

A hollow foot tends to supinate and needs a neutral shoe without support on one side. However a club-/dropped arch foot, or a club-/hollow foot tends to pronate. The latter needs a shoe built up on the inside.

However for the non-professional it is difficult to determine which category his feet belong to. Therefore the general public should make use of an orthopaedic shoemaker, who can easily take impressions of the feet and then undertake the necessary steps to balance the gait.
Stated simply: if a runner knows his exact foot type he has taken the first step towards choosing the correct shoe.

• *Running style*
Most distance runners are heel strikers. With every step they strike the ground with the heel first. They should look out particularly for good shock absorption qualities in the heel area. A forefoot runner needs the cushioning element more in the forefoot area under the ball of the foot.

• *Body weight*
With heavier body weights the running shoe comes under greater strain and the demands for cushioning, stability and durability are greater. A heavy runner will quickly wear out a light running shoe, whereas a lighter runner will find a firm shoe hard and unforgiving. A heavy runner needs a shoe with additional stabilisers and hard wedges in the mid sole. This also applies to women's shoes, although their fit is altered slightly and directed principally at lighter body weights. As a result it is virtually impossible for the male runner to wear women's running shoes, the other way round is more the case. Children and teenagers should look around for something suitable the women's shoes.

• *Underfoot conditions (ground)*
Hard asphalt or concrete necessitates a soft, cushioned running shoe, while uneven, loose ground needs a hard shoe for more support and stability. It is also important that the sole has enough grip, however very rarely does a runner always run on the same ground. Block profiles are better suited to running on the roads, while studded or knotty profiles give more grip on loose ground. Snow also needs a coarse profile to grip, however no shoe can cope on ice.

Although a running shoe is seldom worn for a long period it must be able to cope with all seasons. Certainly a change of shoes according to outside conditions would be best. Although having two or three pairs of shoes to alternate means an enormous initial outlay, there is the advantage that one is better prepared for the weather and underfoot conditions. As already stated, running shoes also need periodic rests.

• *Shoe size*

He, who has already suffered from a black toenail, will pay better attention to the length of the shoe when buying the next pair. However, most people buy their shoes too short, and this does not only apply to sports shoes. A running shoe is only as good as its fit. Unfortunately manufacturers sizing varies causing confusion when buying. Basically, a correctly fitting shoe does not put pressure on the toe from above or at the front. Shoes should always be bought according to the larger foot. One should also consider that the foot swells and broadens under the strain of a long run, and that the toes spread forward in the rolling phase. (Diag. 142)

As models of shoes are made on different lasts this also makes lengths vary. In running shoes there should generally be a gap of a finger width (approx. 1.5 cm) between the longest toe and the end of the toe box. It goes without saying that space also needs to be allowed for running socks. Competition shoes and spikes are worn smaller and more close-fitting. These epitomise better performances and times to most runners. However the lighter weight is only noticeable in a runner who runs, for example, 10 km under 40 minutes. Hence, these shoes are designed for speed at the expense of their durability. Thus these shoes are only needed after 500-700 kilometres in training and are often no good value for money. The lighter weight means softer and less stable materials are used.

Diag. 142:
With increased rolling movement of the foot in the take-off phase the foot does not find enough free room in the toe area, and the big toe rubs at the front and on the top.

In comparison normal running shoes should usually last longer, only wearing out after 1,200 to a maximum of 1,500 kilometres. In the case of pronounced overpronation, however, they can wear out after barely 1,000 km. (Diag 143)

Diag. 144:
A sight not rare in running circles: a clear example of a worn out shoe.

Diag. 143:
After a certain length of time the shoes give way to the tendency of the foot. This compacted mid sole in the mid section is easily recognised.

• *Price-/performance relationship*
Every year the price lists from running shoe manufacturers show that running shoes can cost over £100. With such prices we are not only paying for hightech but also for the labour intensive manufacture. One must pay at least £60 for a decent running shoe. They can be found cheaper but these shoes cannot meet all demands, wearing out after a short time and failing to fulfil basic functions.

In conclusion, choosing the correct shoe is not easy and unfortunately shoe tests in running magazines can also not be relied on.

Tests carried out by neutral parties, or even serious publications, by the manufacturers give only direct information on the purpose, classification, fit and price of a running shoe. An individual assessment which takes the individual biological circumstances into consideration is clearly of better value, than choosing a shoe from a test report.

In spite of this the runner can gain expert knowledge by reading tests and publications and the correct choice of shoe becomes easier later. An up-to-date test table by **Carl-Jürgen Diem** makes this clear. For the final choice the fit, the cushioning, the heel direction and the lacing system are decisive, as the running shoes purchased should be guaranteed for many, hopefully problem free, kilometres.

When trying on one should take enough time, wear the correct socks, try both shoes and where possible try them out on a treadmill or on a 100 m stretch outside the shop if the weather is fine. It can also be useful to show the old worn shoes to an expert in the shop. This gives him the opportunity to recognise the runner's characteristics and identify his training needs.

Recommended Uses for Running Shoes

Make / Model	adidas Falcon (Lady)	adidas SL 96 plus (Lady)	adidas Lexikon Extra (Lady)	Asics Gel-Moto II	Asics Gel-Tarther WG	Asics Gel-GT 2010	Brooks Adrenaline ST (Lady)	Brooks Addiction II	Brooks Radius	Lunge Pulse	Nike Air Streak Light
Well-Trained (faster than 6 min/kil.) <65 kg	+	++	-	+	++	++	+	o	o	++	++
65-80 kg	++	o	+	++	o	++	++	++	+	+	o
>80 kg	-	-	++	o	-	o	+	+	o	-	-
Slow runners / Beginners <65 kg	++	o	-	+	+	++	o	o	o	+	-
>80 kg	o	-	++	o	-	+	++	++	++	-	-
Training/ Long distance races	++	o	++	++	o	++	++	++	++	+	+
Short racing distances (< 20 km)	+	++	+	cross	++	++	++	++	o	++	++
Flat, road running	++	++	++	o	++	+	+	++	++	++	++
Forest runs, uneven ground	+	o	++	++	o	+	o	+	+	o	-
Protection against gravel & sharp stones	+	-	+	o	-	o	+	+	+	o	o
wet; underfoot conditions	o	o	+	++	+	+	o	o	+	+	+
Shape of last	curved	curved	lightly curved	curved	curved	curved	heavily curved	heavily curved	curved	curved	heavily curved
width - forefoot	medium	narrow	broad	medium	narrow	medium	medium	medium	medium	broad	narrow
width - heel	narrow	medium	medium	narrow	narrow	narrow	medium	narrow	medium	medium	narrow
Forefoot -length of toe box	long	normal	short	normal	normal	short	medium	medium	normal	normal	long
Support system - pronation (inner)	o	o	++	++	o	++	++	++	o	+	-
- supination (outer)	o	o	+	o	o	+	+	+	o	-	-
Cushioning during hard heel strike	soft	quite soft	firm	firm	quite soft	quite firm	firm	firm	firm	quite soft	firm
Foot direction	o	+	o	+	+	++	++	++	+	+	+
Stability in forefoot	+	+	+	+	++	++	+	++	++	++	+
Price	£ 49.-	£ 50.-	£ 65.-	£ 60.-	£ 70.-	£ 65.-	£ 55.-	£ 60.-	£ 55.-	£ 60.-	£ 65.-
Remarks	Good value shoe for light to medium weight runners, who do not have pronation problems.	Light training/ racing shoe for light to medium weight runners, without foot problems. Ensure the heel fits well.	Stable training shoe for medium to heavy runners with a good foot directional and support system. The lip on the inside is bulky.	Poor weather shoe for medium weight runners, with good anti-pronation support, particularly on rutted forest paths. Look out for ankle freedom.	Road training shoe for light to medium weight runners, who make good contact with the ground and do not have a pronation problem.	Training/racing shoe for light to medium weight runners with good foot direction. Pronation support good for light weight runners.	Road running shoe for medium weight and heavy runners with good antipronation support and good direction.	Training shoe for medium weight and heavy runners with good antipronation support and good direction.	Comfortable training shoe with good protection against foot roll for medium runners without special support needs.	Light, width adjusted road shoe for light to medium weight runners with support for light to medium pronators.	Light competition shoe for short distances on the road or track.

Classification: ++ very good,/very suitable, + good,/suitable, o average/ok, - not good,/suitable
For Support system: ++ suitable for heavy over pronators, + suitable for medium over pronators, o suitable only for light pronators, - no support system
Price?: These models are also suitable for this target group. Prices over £ 85 excludes a recommendation from me
Lady = Lady-Version tested; (Lady) = Description holds for men's and women's version.

Recommended Uses for Running Shoes

Make / Model	Nike Air Terra Outback	Nike Air Max Tailwind	Puma Trinomic Cushioning II	Puma Trinomic Control II	Puma Cell Distance II	Reebok Voodoo II	Reebok Rebel Road	Reebok Intervall Lady	Saucony GRID Moco (Lady)	Saucony GRID Stabil	Saucony Hurricane
Well-Trained (faster than 6 min/kil.) <65 kg	o	+	+	-	o	o	+	++	+	-	+
65-80 kg	++	+	++	+	++	++	++	++	++	+	++
>80 kg	+	o	+	++	+	o	o	o	+	++	+
Slow runners <65 kg	o	+	+	+	o	o	+	++	-	-	price ?
>80 kg	++	++	++	++	++	+	+	o	++	++	++
Training/Long distance races	++		+	++	++	++	++	++	+	++	++
Short racing distances (< 20 km)	+	+	++	++	+	+	++	++	o	o	+
Flat, road running	+	+	+	++	++	++	+	+	+	+	++
Forest runs, uneven ground	++	-	+	+	++	+	+	o	+	++	+
Protection against gravel & sharp stones	+	+	+	+	+	+	+	o	+	+	+
wet underfoot conditions	+	+	+	+	o	+	+	+	+	++	+
Shape of last	curved	curved	curved	lightly curved	curved	lightly curved	lightly curved	curved	lightly curved	lightly curved	curved
width - forefoot	very wide	medium	wide	wide	wide	narrow	medium	medium	wide	medium	medium
- heel	wide	medium	medium	medium	medium	narrow	narrow	narrow	wide	medium	narrow
Forefoot -length of toe box	short	normal	normal	short	medium	long	medium	short	medium	short	short
Support system - pronation (inner)	++	-	-	++	o	o	o	++	o	+	- -
- supination (outer)	+	-	-	+	o	o	o	+	o	-	- -
Cushioning during hard heel strike	firm	soft	soft	very firm	quite soft	quite soft	medium hard	medium hard	firm	firm	firm
Foot direction	+	o	o	++	+	+	+	+	+	+	++
Stability in forefoot	+	o	+	++	+	o	+	++	+	++	++
Price	£ 75.-	£ 60.-	£ 50.-	£ 40.-	£ 65.-	£ 55.-	£ 50.-	£ 45.-	£ 60.-	£ 60.-	£ 65.-
Remarks	Stable training shoe for medium and heavy runners with good foot direction and support. Above all watch out for a snug heel fit.	Comfortable road shoe for medium and heavy runners at good speeds (clearly under 6 mins/km).	Good value training shoe for medium weight runners without specific support needs.	Very stable shoe for medium to heavy runners, with good foot direction and support, check for a snug heel fit.	Training shoe for medium weight runners looking for a comfortable shoe at slow speeds.	Training shoe for medium weight runners, both slow and fast, with narrow feet.	Simple training shoe for light to medium weight runners at slow speeds, also for heavy runners with narrow feet.	Training-/competition shoe for light to medium weight runners with narrow feet. The shoe is firmer on the supination area than on the inside.	Training shoe for medium weight runners with wide feet. Good anti-pronation support. Check for a snug fit.	Stable training and walking shoe, for medium weight runners (male) and heavy females, with a good support.	Training-/competition shoe for light to medium weight runners with narrow feet, and heavier runners at slower speeds. Good support system.

Classification: ++ very good/very suitable, + good/suitable, o average/ok, - not good/suitable
For Support system: ++ suitable for heavy over pronators, + suitable for medium over pronators, o suitable only for light pronators, - no support system
Price: These models are also suitable for this target group. Prices over £ 85 excludes a recommendation from me
Lady = Lady Version tested; (Lady) = Description holds for men's and women's version.

1.4   Caring for Running Shoes

The shoes should have the opportunity to breathe after every training run or competition, as the foot sweats heavily while running. The material used is usually synthetic and does not allow enough air through nor moisture out. Therefore, shoes should be stored in a dry, warm in winter, place. Direct contact with heaters or ovens would, however, dry out and damage the materials, especially damaging the outer and mid soles. The same goes for the summer, shoes should not be placed in direct sunlight as this can loosen the adhesives.

When the shoe becomes wet inside during rain the insole should be removed and laid to dry, ensuring that it does not become bent or damaged. Then the shoe should be stuffed with paper, to absorb a large proportion of the water. After removing the paper allow the shoes to dry at room temperature. If shoes are left wet, especially under the insole, then mould develops, causing odour. Occasionally powder the dry insole and inside of the shoe with an antibacterial powder to neutralise odours, to stop problems such as athletes' foot developing.

If the shoes become very soiled all-round care is necessary. The sole can be rubbed with a wet sponge. It is however forbidden to use washing detergents to clean. All normal detergents are too harsh, even hand washing detergents. They attack and dry out the mid sole area, making it brittle. Specially designed sports shoe shampoos are better for cleaning the shoes. Washing in machines should not be done above 30 degrees. Finally the shoes must be dried. This takes up to three days, according to the weather, as the shoe material retains a lot of water.

2.   Improved Running Shoes

2.1   The Relationship between Foot and Shoe

Many problems with the Achilles' tendon, lower and upper leg muscles, knees and vertebrae are caused through running in ill-fitting or worn out shoes, that do not or can no longer fulfil their basic functions. The feet and the running shoes must build a unit. In this way the foot is comfortable and protected whilst running. When the feet are wrongly loaded and unsuitable shoes cannot compensate for, or even worsen, the abnormal foot stance and actions, then overuse injuries result. For example: a stable running shoe, with corrective stability on the inside of the shoe will protect the runner who has a tendency to pronate from injury. The same shoe would force a runner with hollow foot and a tendency to supinate to land further on the outside – possibly damaging the outer ligaments. If the support system of a shoe is not sufficient to balance the foot problems then an orthopaedic shoe specialist should be consulted. Using a treadmill analysis he can adapt and correct the conventional shoes to suit. In this way harmony between the foot and shoe is achieved.

After extensive running the athlete needs to give his feet time to recover, and this needs to be in comfortable shoes. When one thinks how much money one spends on running shoes, one has to ask why runners do not ensure that they wear comfortable shoes during the time spent away from running. Everyday shoes should always be comfortable. For women, especially, choosing shoes is a fashion aspect which seldom works out to the advantage of the feet. (Diag. 48) However, when the foot is forced into an unnatural position it is put at risk of injury as a result of undue strain. Proper fitting street shoes come as a great relief on long work days and represent a worthwhile investment.

2.2   Treadmill Analysis and Electronic Plantar Pressure Measurements

A video treadmill analysis serves as a good method of discovering foot faults and optimising running style and motion. Hence it provides a way of avoiding injury. In the past this was attempted by filming athletes running outside, this was however unreliable, difficult and costly. For this reason, more than fifteen years ago, treadmills already well tried in rehabilitation therapy, were deployed to monitor running techniques. This method provides a way of detecting problems of the wrong load of the foot thus facilitating the correct choice of running shoe. Every orthopaedic shoemaker who specialises in sports orthopaedics should use such a treadmill as an essential piece of diagnostic equipment. He can use it to diagnose the errors in body statics which can lead to problems in the feet, joints and muscles, and put the necessary corrections in place. The recorded running is analysed in slow motion and discussed with the athlete undergoing the analysis. (Diag. 145)

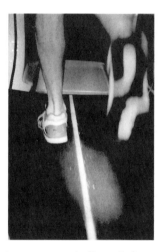

Diag. 145:
The treadmill analysis enables the recognition of faults in the different stages of running and the recommendation of the most suitable shoes. In the photograph this tendency to pronate in the left foot can be fully corrected with improved shoes.

A proper treadmill analysis, and above all a good evaluation of the results, is only possible if the orthopaedic specialist carrying out the test is properly qualified.

A profound knowledge of the anatomy, structure and biomechanics of the body, in connection with an understanding of the sporting aspect, is vital. Unfortunately very few have this requisite training, and even fewer have running studios at their disposal in which to carry out exact controls.

An electronic plantar pressure measurement is a very powerful tool that is however seldom used in sport. This involves placing a measuring insole in the shoe, which takes the individual impression of the foot and evaluates it through a computer. The values taken of the individual's pressure over the foot area clearly highlight areas of greater pressure, and measures can be taken to minimise this stress. Originally developed as a way of assessing the feet of diabetics, the method has been used in sport to provide a clear answer to questions about the shape of finished orthosis or the effectiveness of measures to correct shoes. Unfortunately this procedure is very costly and for this reason payment is currently not always met by the health insurance companies.

While a treadmill analysis is reliant on the optical attention and competence of the tester, the electronic impression system can give a precise analysis of areas stressed and even bring a quantitative element to the correction of the shoes.

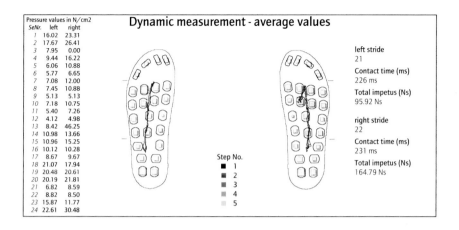

Diag. 146:
Printout 1:
Shows the dynamic measurement of standard running shoes with normal insoles when jogging (running)

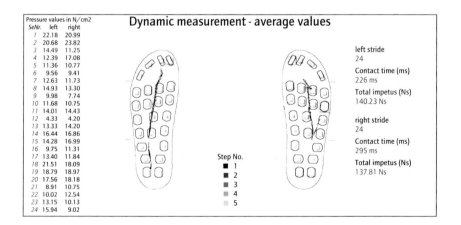

Printout 2:
Shows the same situation, this time with special sports inserts (orthosis) at the same speed. The distribution of the load in the mid foot is clear, as is the reduction of pressure on the fifth metatarsal bones.

2.3   Sports Orthosis

Many athletes mistakenly refer to the inlays in their running shoes as the footbed. The task of these inlays is simply to even out and cover up irregularities in the base of the inner shoe. On the upper side the inlay is covered with an absorbent material which is softer in the heel area, however it does not fulfil any support function. Conventional orthosis should not be used in sport. Their function is to correct and support the foot in everyday street shoes. However they are harder and less flexible than sports orthosis. In the latter softer synthetic materials are used and preferably combined with the harder materials.

Sports orthosis are designed to support and direct the foot during long periods of stress to try and stop the muscles getting overtired and avoid the increased foot faults and running faults which are caused by this tiredness. They are not designed to have a corrective effect on the form of the foot itself. Additional cushioning through the inserts is not intended. Sports orthosis should always be made for the individual after measurement or by taking an impression of the foot. The individuality of such orthosis is immediately noticeable upon wearing them. Not only do they raise the comfort for the wearer, they also optimise the running motion and stance of the runner, particularly during long runs.

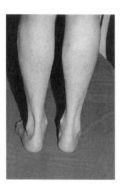 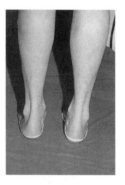 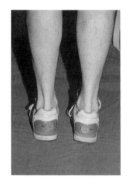

Diag. 147 a:
The left foot is pronating badly. The runner suffers from overuse problems in the left ankle joint after running.

Diag. 147 b:
The specifically made sports orthosis only partially correct this fault but ...

Diag 147 c:
... in connection with the correct type of running shoe this faulty foot stance is fully corrected.

Medical insurance schemes only cover the cost of sports orthosis if these are medically necessary. The shape and the structure of the orthosis, and also the materials used, vary according to the problems and the basic needs of the athlete. For example, different orthosis can help to overcome pronation problems, relieve problems of "Hallux-Rigidus", alleviate the pressure of plantarfasciitis by using a softer covering, and relieve burning forefoot sensations by providing the necessary support. (Diag. 147)

Sports orthosis need to be worn in. It is fundamentally wrong to use new orthosis immediately for a long training session. It is recommended that, to begin with, you only wear the new orthosis (in your running shoes) around the house for a few hours at a time. The reason for this lies in the soft upper surfaces, which take a few hours of pressure to fully achieve their correct shape and fulfil their correct functions.

2.4   Modification of Running Shoes

As with normal street shoes orthopaedic corrective modification of running shoes can help with leg and foot problems. The basic consideration when altering a running shoe is that a better stance is achieved and the comfort of the runner increased. When necessary the alteration of a running shoe can even out a leg length discrepancy, thus relieving tendons or joints.

A leg length discrepancy can be equalised in several ways depending upon the extent of the discrepancy. Up to 0.6 cm of difference can be balanced by fixing the necessary amount of flexible, yet durable, material to the inlay of the shoe. If the leg length discrepancy is in addition to another foot problem then the sports orthosis rather than the shoe inlay should be adapted. (Diag. 148) With a pronounced leg length difference (between 1 and 1.5 cm) then an extra mid sole should be added. (Diag. 149) In order not to change the nature of the running shoe the mid sole must be made from the same flexible material. Not every running shoe lends itself to alteration, and this needs to be kept in mind when buying. Ultimately the advice of a sports orthopaedic specialist should be sought.

Diag. 148:
Leg length discrepancy up to 1 cm can be equalised by specially made sports orthosis.

Diag 149:
Larger length discrepancies (between 1 and 1.5 cm) need to be balanced by externally added shoe mid soles. The corrected left shoe has had the inner edge raised, while the right has been raised to equalise a leg lenght problem.

A minor foot stance fault can be corrected by adapting the shoe (i.e. with pronation support). However with pronounced foot stance problems sports orthosis must be used. The correction of running shoes by raising either the outside or the inside edge of the shoe or by raising the whole shoe to balance a leg length difference is just as possible with ready-made shoes. The effect of the finished shoe correction should finally be checked by using a treadmill control. Height and correction values given by manufacturers should only be carried over to the running shoes with care. Since all steps are almost the same when running, too much correction can quickly lead to overuse problems.

Diag. 150:
Raising the inner edge of the mid sole gives an improved stance in the knee and ankle joints in the case of X-legs.

Diag. 151:
Placing a flexible wedge under the heel can reduce the strain on the Achilles' tendon during running.

3. Foot Exercises and Foot Care

Good and comfortable footwear allows our foot muscles (particularly the short muscles on the sole of the foot) to waste away, since they are no longer required to carry out their intended functions. Barefoot beach running, on sand or on shingle, on holiday is not enough to avoid faulty foot plants, which can eventually lead to stance problems (such as club-foot, fallen arches and splay foot). Only daily foot exercises can work against this and build up the lazy foot muscles (see following diagrams).

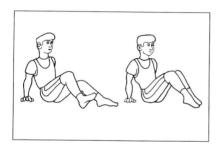

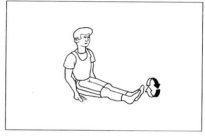

Diag. 152:
Bending and stretching the foot in a squatting position.

Diag. 153:
Circling the feet when sitting legs outstretched.

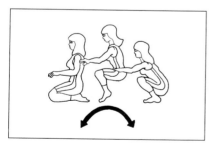

Diag 154:
Sitting back on the heels: stretches the feet
- bending the feet
- squatting onto the soles of the feet.

Diag. 155:
In the kneeling press-up position: stretching and flexing the feet.

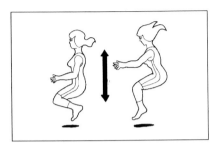

Diag. 156:
Springing and jumping in the squatting position.

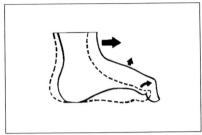

Diag. 157:
Caterpillar walking

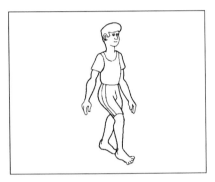

Diag. 158:
Spreading out the toes while walking barefoot.

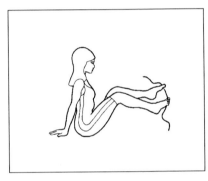

Diag. 159:
Alternatively picking up a line or rope with the toes.

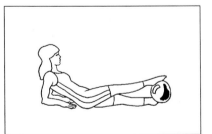

Diag. 160:
Holding a ball with the feet.

Diag. 161:
Tearing newspapers apart with the feet and toes.

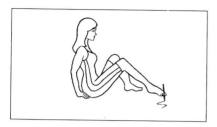

Diag. 162:
Drawing with the feet.

Diag. 163:
Gripping pebbles with the toes and moveing from pile to pile.

Not only can problems be solved by new shoes or sports orthosis, often it is only a case of small problems which can be easily swept aside by good foot care.

• **The build-up of blisters** is caused by an increased mechanical irritation, or rubbing on the skin from outside. This can come about through pressure or twisting. Caring for this problem with plasters only leads to increased pressure and less room in the shoe. However, there are situations where no improvement is possible despite various modifications to the running shoe. The problem is probably with the skin itself. A dry skin can only stand a limited amount of twisting or pressure. Thus moisturising cream or grease should be worked into the skin, particularly in the affected area. In order to avoid blisters whilst running, many distance runners rub their toes with vaseline or creams prior to running.

• Patches of hard skin or calluses are a particular problem for the feet. The causes are usually pressure or rubbing points caused by faulty foot plant or stance (see chpt. IV. 15). Sanding down, pumice stones and chemicals only temporarily tackle the problem and this only with decreasing efficiency. A callus is a whitish layer of dead skin which serves as a biological protection against the pressure or irritation at the particular point. The reason for this irritation or pressure must be established. If the cause lies with a faulty foot plant or stance, then a specialist doctor should be consulted. When the problem is faulty shoes, changing or correcting the shoes will bring relief to the runner.

• Cracked or chapped feet can be easily dealt with. They come about if the skin is too dry, particularly in the stressed areas of the foot sole. Creams or greases for chapped skin bring relief. If a runner continues to experience minor problems whilst pursuing his sport it would be advisable to seek foot care treatment from a chiropodist.

4. Thermoregulation

In order to "Optimise Your Running" it is not only necessary to look after your health. The athlete should also function according to his heat balance. Every runner knows that his muscles can only work successfully when they are sufficiently warmed-up. However, they must not get overheated. The body requires an optimal temperature to be maintained.

4.1 Terms and Biological Explanation

The term 'body temperature' relates to the physiologically influenced temperature which rules internally in our bodies – particularly in the brain. In the middle of the day the average man has a normal body temperature of 36.8 degrees C, which fluctuates around 1 to 1.5 degrees C according to the time of day. It reaches a minimum in the morning and peaks in the afternoon. (Diag. 164):

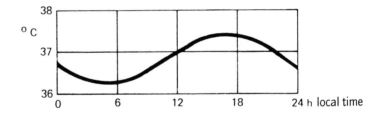

Diag. 164: Daily fluctuation of body temperature (from Marées, Horst de: Sportphysiologie, 8. corrected new edition, p. 287, Sport & Buch Strauß, Cologne 1996)

In women the average body temperature can sometimes be around 0.5 degrees C higher, when hormonal influences are also at work. Fluctuations of more than 4 degrees C in core body temperature mean a reduction in physical and mental capabilities. Such large fluctuations consequently bring increased damage; extreme changes damage the sensitive body cells and can eventually lead to death.

The regulation of temperature, or thermoregulation, refers to the efforts of the body to maintain and regulate its optimal temperature through changing external conditions. Sports physiology identifies two different ways of achieving this. Firstly, the human body is naturally capable of keeping the temperature of its individual parts – above all its core – constant, despite changes in external conditions. Secondly, the individual has, since primeval times, willingly supported his body's efforts by clothing himself appropriately.

4.2   Natural Thermoregulation

In the body shell, especially the extremities, the body temperature is low, especially on the skin. Whether a part of the body belongs to the body core or shell, depends on the surrounding condition, as Diag. 165 shows:

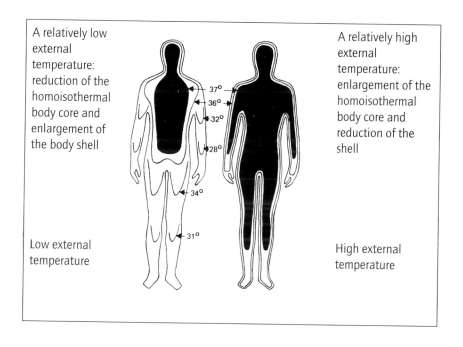

A relatively low external temperature: reduction of the homoisothermal body core and enlargement of the body shell

37°
36°
32°
28°
34°
31°

A relatively high external temperature: enlargement of the homoisothermal body core and reduction of the shell

Low external temperature

High external temperature

Diag. 165:
Various sizes of body shell and body core under different external temperatures (Aschoff J. et al. „Energiehaushalt und Thermoregulation" Bd. 2.
In: Gauer/Kramer/Jung: Physiologie der Menschen, Urban & Schwarzenberg Verlag, Munich 1971).

In order to keep the core body temperature constant humans possess corresponding sensors in the temperature regulating centre of the inter-brain. These, together with temperature sensors on the surface of the skin – principally responsible for external cooling – control the temperature regulating centre in the inter-brain. From here all regulating mechanisms are set in motion.

4.2.1   Effects of the Cold

If the surrounding temperature drops and there is not enough warmth available, then the body automatically concentrates on maintaining its core temperature in the essential parts of the body (see Diag. 165), while allowing all other parts to cool. This defence mechanism is known as centralisation. Finally, all that remains are the inner parts of the head and torso, and only here is the specific temperature maintained.

A further measure used by the body to fight against cold is shivering. This raises metabolism and heat generation. At the same time the skin temperature and heat exchange improve through better convection into the surrounding air. Hence this counter measure is not particularly effective.

On the other hand all chemical reactions in the body are limited if, for example, the muscles are too cold. As a consequence little warmth is produced since the metabolic process only functions slowly. In this case the body's capabilities are limited. When the muscles are below temperature even the pain threshold is lowered. Thus the risk of injury and the danger of generally overextending the body are greater.

The cold also worsens the physical condition of the joints. During movement the supply of nutrients and the work of the cartilage to clear harmful substances via the fluids in the joints are slowed down. Thus the joints stiffen. With today's knowledge running in low or even freezing temperatures when dressed in shorts and T-shirts should not be considered!

With this background knowledge it becomes clear that the stretching exercises previously highlighted should only be undertaken when the muscles are sufficiently warm. – All in all we must accept that the adjustment of the body to cope with the cold costs a great deal of energy, and this detracts from sporting performance. Therefore the runner needs to dress accordingly.

4.2.2   Effects of Heat

At rest the human body produces excess heat. During basal metabolism the body burns 0.3 g/hour of oxygen, giving a heat surplus of 250-380 kj (60-90 kcal). This amount must be got rid of, and there are several ways of achieving this:

- through convection/conduction
- through radiation
- through vaporisation/evaporation.

At 20°C and resting, the amounts of heat leaving the body by various means are about the same. Under different conditions, however, they can vary greatly, as Figure 166 shows

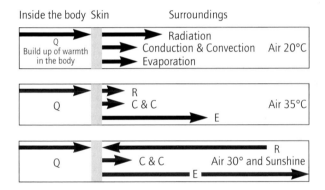

Diag. 166:
Heat flows from the body under various conditions (from Hensel)
(Length of the arrow = size of heat flow; from de Mareés: Sportphysiologie, p. 296)

Thus, higher air temperatures and sunshine, for example, can cause the radiation heat flows to be reversed, and the necessary cooling must be carried out almost entirely through evaporation.

The stresses and strains placed on the body, above all by endurance athletes, produce enormous warmth in the body, particularly in the muscles. According to the effort more than 75% (maximum of up to 97%) of the energy turnover is converted into heat. It relies, therefore, especially in high external temperatures, on sweat evaporation to prevent the body from overheating. Approximately two million sweat droplets help to ensure that up to 3 l/h are eliminated from the pores and evaporate from the skin thus cooling the surface. Yet, aside from the sweat droplets, the skin also allows quite a lot of water to vaporise, and the air circulation also helps to dissipate the huge amounts of heat which are around 17,000 kj/h (4,000 kcal/h). The lower the air temperature and the stronger the air circulation, the higher the proportion of heat lost through radiation and convection.

4.2.3   Transportation of Heat within the Body

When the body is working, and during strenuous training, the heat production rises to as much as fifteen times the level produced when the body is at rest. Thus considerably larger amounts of heat must be transported around the body. At first the warmth produced by the work in the muscles is used by the muscles in order to keep themselves warm. As a result the temperature of the muscles rises from 34 to 40 degrees (warm-up training). Only after this does a flow of heat build up, transported by the blood to other areas of the body.

After the whole body has reached this warmer temperature, the blood flow to the skin is increased and the body begins transporting the heat to the surrounding atmosphere. While at rest the body releases around 40% of the excess heat into the atmosphere; during work or sporting effort the proportion released drops to around 10% of the considerably higher total.

The circulation to the skin provides the temperature regulating system with a sensitive instrument of enormous potential. Circulation through the fingers alone can increase to a maximum of 600 fold.

4.3   Supporting Thermoregulation

Since the body can only tolerate a core temperature kept within the narrow range of 36.3 to 37.5 degrees C and the capabilities of natural regulation within the human body cannot achieve this in harsh external conditions, the athlete must rely on appropriate dressing. He must observe the rules for maintaining the correct temperature in the lower part of the body as well as the upper section. Here he is supported by modern developments in textile physiology, the understanding of the relationships between the human body, the climate and clothing.

Basically the clothing must be able to fulfil certain functions; and for the endurance athlete these can be extreme. This has lead to the recent coining of the term "functional clothing". Today the magical "function" word is used everywhere and bluntly misused in advertising. As we will proceed to show it is in fact very difficult and costly to develop and guarantee truly functional items.

On the other hand it is not sufficient - as the literature points out from time to time – simply to advise the athlete, in order for him to gain a comprehensive overview and finally to be able to choose the correct clothing for his sporting discipline. This would be the equivalent of a devoted mother sending her child out to school in the morning through the dangerously busy city traffic armed only with the insistent, yet too general reminder: be careful!!

One must therefore explain to those runners, who are not yet sufficiently experienced and knowledgeable, exactly which is the correct clothing. In the following section the authors have set out to achieve this.

4.3.1   Clothing Demands

The correct functional clothing should open up the way for the runner to optimise his running. They must isolate him and keep him warm in cold weather, protect him from the wet, get rid of perspiration during endurance running, protect the athlete from burning sun rays and yet, in spite of this, avoid heat building up. During recovery breaks in training, and in cold winds, the body should not be allowed to get cold. - All these requirements appear to contradict each other when one does not consider that one item of clothing does not have to fulfil all the criteria.

4.3.2   Heat Transportation to the Outside

Excess body heat can only be got rid of through sweating if the moisture can vaporise from the skin. If this is possible then 2,452 kj (=586 kcal) per litre are used to convert this moisture into a gaseous state.

At a skin temperature of 35 degrees C this process does not occur quantitatively (which is why it is better to refer to evaporation), instead there are some warmer water molecules which transfer to a gas state, while some colder molecules remain stuck on the skin as moisture. The higher the temperature of the skin, the higher the proportion of gaseous particles and therefore the more pleasant the conditions for the athlete under the clothing.

This means, however that the space directly above the skin and its sweat droplets, must be kept at an optimal temperature, i.e. well-isolated and sufficiently ventilated. However contradictory it may sound our skin must be kept warm enough to keep itself cool, i.e. so that it can sufficiently get rid of excess heat. Textile specialists talk of the micro climate above the surface of the skin, which, for comfort, should be as dry as possible.

Such a relationship is best achieved when the inner side of the layer of textile nearest to the skin has a structured surface with raised fibres pointed inwards.

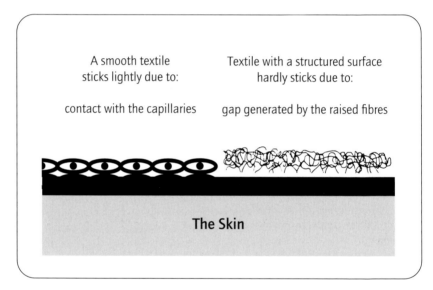

Diag. 167:
The smooth fabric made from absorbent filament threads (left) sticks to the sweaty damp skin through the capillary effect, while textiles with more open structures and raised fibres (right) create a drier, more pleasant micro climate. (Jürgen Mecheels: Körper – Klima – Kleidung, picture 43, p. 87, Verlag Schiele & Schön GmbH, Berlin 1991)

The liquid sweat particles need to be cleared away in order that they do not remain on the skin undoing the so-called cool-back effect with their unpleasant consequences. That is the task facing the textured fabrics with their specially structured surfaces.

4.4   A Small Matter of Materials

One basic difference between natural fibres and synthetically manufactured chemical fibres is apparent in their reactions to water. Natural fibres such as wool or cotton have a hydrophile surface (which attracts water).

Chemical fibres, however, generally have a hydrophobic surface, i.e. they repel water. Alongside their many good qualities natural fibres have the disadvantage of absorbing and storing the moisture.

The transportation of sweat hardly occurs, and this is decisive for the endurance athlete's choice of clothing. Cotton, above all, tends to soak up moisture, eventually bringing the sweat transportation to a standstill.

Hence, the decision between natural and synthetic fibres falls clearly on the side of the synthetics. Their advantages are so overwhelming that, even in Germany, the prejudices of the ecological and natural fibre movements have been widely dispelled. Now the chemical industry can produce the synthetic fibres made to measure, so to speak. This means the individual qualities can be adapted to suit the individual purposes. To this end, attention must be paid to – alongside the choice of the correct raw materials – the construction of the threads, whether joins are knitted or woven, and even the particular cut of each item of clothing.

Only the correct combination of all four influences enables the manufacture of truly functional textiles.

4.4.1   Which Synthetic Fibres?

In the past twenty years there has been a lot of experimentation. Almost every big manufacturer of synthetic fabrics has developed his product further, achieving a level which will satisfy most demands. A scarcely imaginable series of trials should be undertaken in the physiological clothing laboratories in order to achieve clarity in the physical context.

For the distance runner clothing must above all be relied upon to get rid of the sweat, without retaining to any extent any moisture over long periods. The following graphic illustrates how the modern synthetics fare in this respect:

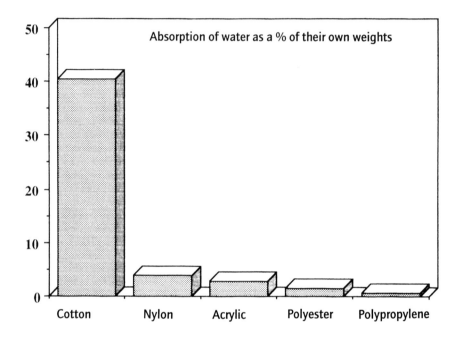

Diag. 168:
Absorbency of moisture of different synthetic fibres when compared with cotton.

Polyester and polypropylene have the lowest absorbency of moisture as against their own body weight. However, both nylon and acrylic are also under 5% and are therefore basically appropriate to be used for clothing worn next to the skin.

A further, less important criterion lies in the heat conductive capabilities of the fibre. Here the demand is that it be as low as possible in order that the isolation effect of the layer nearest to the skin is not lost.

Table 3 shows the heat conductive capacities of the materials in question:

Fibre	Heat conductive capacity
Polypropylene	6.0
Polyvinyl chloride	6.4
Polyester	7.0
Wool	7.3
Acrylic	8.0
Cotton	17.5

Table 3: Heat conductive capacities of the most important fibres

With respect to this quality, polypropylene and polyester again come out on top. However, the workability of the fibre appears more important. If a fibre can be drawn out very thinly, then it is possible to make a tissue which is quite dense with very good isolation qualities.

Earlier natural silk, with a fibre strength of approx. 1 dtex, was unsurpassable in the areas of isolation effects and comfort of wearing. 1 dtex (or Dezitex) means that 10,000 m of the fibre weighs 1 gram. Modern synthetic fibres can be spun much finer than silk, while at the same time they can also be spun as coarse fibres. The possibilities that this offers are shown in Diag. 169:

Fibre	Range of fineness in dtex	Micro-fibres	Finest fibre, fine fibres	Coarse fibres
			1 2 3 4 5 6 7 8 9 10 11 12 13 14 15 16 17 18 19	
			Fibre fineness in dtex	
Cotton	1...4			
Linen	10...40			
Wool, hair	2 ...50			
Silk	1...4			
Viscose	1...22			
Acetate	2...10			
Polyester	0,6...44			
Nylon	0,8...22			
Acrilic	0,6...25			
Polypropylen	1,5...40			
Elastane	20..5000		Enlarged 250 times.	

Diag 169: Structure of fibres and the fineness of various natural and synthetic fibres (from „Fachwissen Bekleidung" p. 44, 4th edition, Verlag Europa Lehrmittel – Noumey, Vollmer GmbH & Co., Haan-Gruiten)

In order to get rid of the liquid sweat particles we must again use some physical concepts: droplets of moisture pass by diffusion through the pores of the textile between the woven threads, along the stitching or between the threaded fibres. Physically bonded forces on the surface of the fibres (adsorption) attract the droplets, which then travel along the fibres to the outside, here desorption finally occurs as the moisture evaporates. This transport process becomes more efficient as the total surface of the fibres increases, i.e. it is clearly more efficient with micro fibres.

In this respect two of the modern synthetic fibres are clearly highlighted. As Diag. 169 impressively shows, polyester and acrylic can be spun to 0.6 dtex, which is almost twice as fine as the finest natural fibre. For different areas of usage the same materials can be used to achieve fibre diameters of 50-100 times this.

Since the ability of the fibre capillaries (fine tubes) to take up moisture only works up to the point of saturation, this has not been very successful in endurance sports. Dehydrated capillary bonds between the fibres or finely interwoven gaps are more reliable. The transportation of the sweat is thus decisively influenced by the fineness of the fibres, the pull of the threads and the tightness of the weave.

4.4.2   Structures of the Fibres, Thread and Weave

The next diagram sets out simply the different ways in which the individual staple or infinite fibres (filaments) can be woven or threaded. It gets one thinking how a combination of the individual examples, all from various basic materials, can lead to such a spectrum of possibilities. Each has individual qualities, even more so when subjected to different follow up treatments.

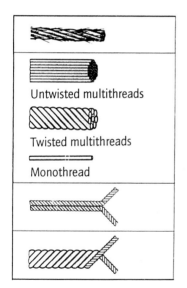

Untwisted multithreads

Twisted multithreads

Monothread

Woven spun fibres from staple fibres which have been twisted together.

Filament weave from untwisted infinite fibres (filaments).

Multithreaded weave from numerous twisted filaments.

Monothread weave from an individual filament.

Flat weave, not twisted together, only wound together.

Strong yarn, threads twisted together.

Diag. 170: Fibres, weaves and yarns; terms from the textile industry (from „Fachwissen Bekleidung", p. 47, Verlag Europa Lehrmittel – Noumey, Vollmer GmbH & Co., Haan-Gruiten)

Diagrams 171 and 172 show all the different ways in which the filaments can be woven.

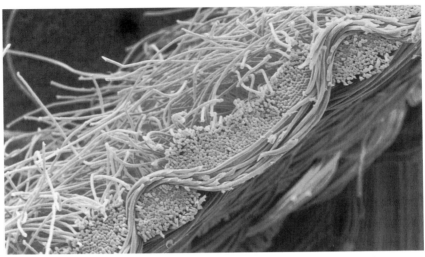

Diag. 171:
Materials woven from polyester possess wind and water resistance together with good breathability (thanks to the generous support of Hoechst Trevira KG, Frankfurt/Main).

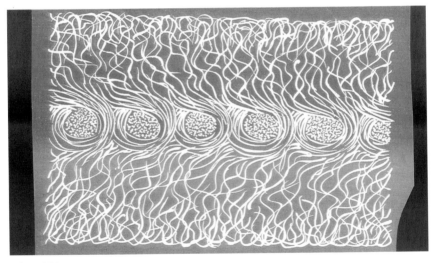

Diag. 172:
Fleece weave with excellent heat isolation qualities (thanks to the generous support of Hoechst Trevira KG, Frankfurt/Main)

It is clear that specific further work can result in the introduction of definite qualities into the fabrics produced.

Many design features can also influence the transportation of moisture through the fabric. The different methods by which this is achieved are laid out in Table 4:

Manner	Type of design	Chemical/ synthetic fibre	Type of equipment	thread	Design of textile	cut
diffusion of vapour				X	X	
absorption/ migration	(X)		X	X	X	X
absorption/ desorption	X		(X)		(X)	
transport via capillaries	(X)		X	X	X	
convection/ ventilation			~		X	X

Table 4: Dependency of the individual methods of fluid transportation on the different design features of the textiles. X means stronger dependency, (X) denotes a less marked influence.

Without going into great details it is clear that the design of the textile and clothing, influenced by the levels of surface moisture on the fibres, the way in which the fibres are spun, the design of the weave and stitching as well as the general equipment of the textiles, is essential to the ability to let the moisture through.

4.5   Transportation of Sweat through the Clothing

Up until now the correlations and interrelations are still easily comprehensible. To sum up provisionally: the surface of our skin should, as far as possible, convert the sweat into a gaseous state, which must then be further transported outwards, remaining as far as possible in a gaseous state without being allowed to condense.

Liquid sweat is nevertheless reliably wicked away through kinetic reasons, and because over time more moisture is isolated (held in the fibre) than vaporised, so long as it does not have a role to play in cooling the body.

Diag. 173 serves to make the physical interrelations even clearer:

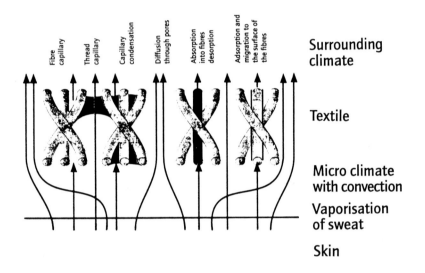

Diag. 173: Possible paths of the water vapour through textiles. (Jürgen Meechels: „Körper – Klima – Kleidung" pict. 29, p. 57, Verlag Schiele & Schön GmbH, Berlin)

Sweat has four possible ways of passing vertically through fibre:

a) Diffusion of the water vapour from the inside to the outside via the air through the pores of the material (shown in the centre of the diagram). This occurs irrespective of the material of the fibres.

b) Adsorption to the surface of the fibres, migration along the fibres, desorption on the outside (far right of the diagram).

c) Transportation of the moisture as liquid through fibre and thread capillaries, and as capillary condensation (options on the left of the diagram), and finally evaporation on the outside.

d) Absorption inside the fibres, transportation through the fibre material, desorption and evaporation from the outer layer of the textile (right of the centre).

When looked at quantitatively mechanisms a) to c) are of great importance for the synthetic textiles, while the absorptive path of d) is generally a characteristic found in materials made from natural fibres.

On the outer surface of the clothing the gaseous molecules usually condense to form droplets, providing the external temperature is not too high. Here they unite with the particles transported as liquid and evaporate into the airflow.

In low temperatures, however, the isolation effect of one single item of clothing is frequently not sufficient. In this case at least a second layer is necessary to maintain body temperature. Here fleece material is favoured, with its micro fibres interwoven to trap the air and thus isolate the body particularly well. In extreme weather conditions, such as strong and cold winds and/or rain, a third layer must be added. This is a protective layer on the outside to protect as far as possible against the effects of the cold and the wet.

In this three layered system the inner layer should ideally provide a micro climate, directly next to the skin, which is as dry as possible. The middle layer needs to provide the necessary insulation without allowing too much sweat condensation, and the outer layer protects against the wind and the weather.

This latter criterion in particular hits physical problems in fulfilling the demands of reliable sweat transportation to the outside. Diagram 174 sets out the ideal scenario diagramatically without going over the transport paths already mentioned:

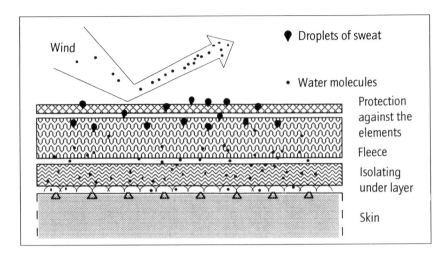

Diag. 174: Diagram of the three layered system of thermoregulation

Sweat vaporises on the skin, supported by the good insulation of the first layer. The gaseous water particles pass through the middle layer of insulation, and does not condense until it reaches the outer surface. Here the problems arise: the outer layer must be dense enough to stop the water droplets (so the rain does not get in), yet porous enough to allow the water molecules (the gaseous sweat) through.

Only in advertisements does such a system function perfectly. Consider that a reasonably densely weave allows approximately 5,500 g of steam per square metre through over 24 hours. When the body sweats heavily 10-20 times this level needs to pass through, and, with data such as this, this appears impossible.

Despite this, the advertisement's promise; that a porous, extremely thin layer of film can act as a one way street, sounds convincing. Yet, what happens to the sweat in droplet form, which must follow the same path to the outside as the vapour? What happens at the dense layer of film where only molecular water can pass through?

It raises the question of whether all the problems of the expectant runner are yet solved. It is more than likely that he must accept a few compromises and be prepared for a few deficiencies in the items he purchases. Hence perfect breathability of an item of clothing and absolute density against wind and rain are, for the moment, mutually exclusive, however, for the runner this is seldom a serious problem.

A performance orientated runner would not choose a watertight layer which, due to its poor breathability, limited his success. It is preferable to him to maximise his performance whilst becoming moist from the rain rather than from his sweat.

4.6   Practical Applications for the Runner

In his quest to optimise his running the ambitious athlete will have drawn the following conclusions from the previous chapter:
    In training and in competition the primary concern is to exploit the natural thermo-regulative ability of the body as far as possible. This is easily achievable in comfortably warm external temperatures and relatively low humidity. Here the body is sufficiently protected by a pair of shorts and a simple T-shirt made from one's favourite material. Even the traditional cotton is ok here, so long as the run lasts no longer than 30-60 mins and is hardly interrupted. A T-shirt must fulfil certain conditions; liquid sweat particles must be absorbed and allowed to spread over the outer surface so they can evaporate easily. In higher temperatures a net shirt is enough, as long as the sun is not too strong; if this is the case then protective clothing is necessary. (It goes without saying that women, due to the female anatomy, also need a good undersupport when running.)

With today's knowledge the recommendation of certain authors for male runners to simply run without shirts in temperatures in excess of 21 degrees C, and to enjoy the refreshing feeling, must be dismissed as dangerous. The same goes for the advice to continue running in shorts unless the temperature drops below zero.

Through such ignorance of the fundamental basics of thermoregulation the runner can do himself lasting harm. The same goes for the habit of replacing a conscientious warm-up with a few precompetition stretching exercises. By doing this the runner risks drawn out muscle and tendon injuries for the sake of saving a few minutes. Whenever possible stretching belongs at the end of the sporting activity when the whole body is thoroughly warm!

Supportive thermoregulation depends on individual physical, climatic and sporting conditions. For this reason we can (unfortunately) only make general recommendations. This is already apparent in the individual's tendency to sweat. For example: one of the authors sweats only on his 'top half', while another hardly ever sweats. Hence the functional clothing can produce highly variant experiences.

Personal experiences are also not to be relied upon. However, in general we question the previously much used rule that a runner should use a costly expensive pair of shoes, yet wear clothing that is as cheap or as old as possible. With today's knowledge this rule can at best only be applied to short, unproblematic, training runs, and is certainly not conducive to good performances in competitions. These are best achieved by wearing carefully chosen functional clothing, which has been individually tried out.

This can at times be a highly costly process, especially if the runner does not receive the correct explanations and advice. In every case the correct choice is a polyester T-shirt which is not too tightly fitted, made from microfleece in a spun-fibre design. Whether suitable leg clothing is necessary is best decided by the individual. In extreme cold the under shirt should be long-sleeved, and complemented by an isolating jumper, also polyester, or a knitted microfleece jacket. These items of clothing must provide good ventilation, i.e. they must allow the air from the outside atmosphere, and the air trapped between the clothing, to circulate as the wearer moves, in order that the water vapours and heat can be transported to the outside.

The final layer of protection against the weather is determined by the climatic conditions and the demands of the type of endurance sport. For running there are some types of windproof material that are sufficiently breathable and can stand up to two hour long runs in the rain without allowing the body to overheat or get too cold. In all cases the runner should favour an effective removal or wicking away of body moisture above total protection against the wet. The body naturally does not remain totally dry, excess sweat together with the rain which does get through accounts for this.

Unfortunately such a process of selection demands time, and certainly the materials described here cannot be found cheaply today, and are not standard equipment for most athletes. If they were then the price would become increasingly cheaper. For this to happen also requires a great deal of effort in the fibre and clothing industries, and a rethinking process for a lot of athletes.

Those however for whom expenditure on modern functional clothing is not too great get increased comfort and – when used correctly – improved sporting performances in return, together with the knowledge that they are doing as much as is presently possible to maintain the health of their bodies.

All in all, however, this makes considerable progress along the path to "Optimise Your Running".

5. Training Guidance According to Biological Parameters

5.1 Biological Basics

The energy for sporting performances comes from burning carbohydrates and fats. This metabolic process can happen in two ways:

1. During great effort the oxygen supply from the air breathed in is not sufficient for the body to burn carbohydrates (anaerobic metabolism). As a result a product is left behind in the body tissues and the blood – lactate. An increase in the amount of lactate in the blood (this can be measured) leads to an overburdening of the body and to a drop off in performance right up until exhaustion.

2. If the sporting activity is carried out at lower intensities, so that the amount of oxygen breathed in is sufficient for the oxidation of the carbohydrates (aerobic metabolism), then the blood lactate levels do not rise. In this case, after 30-40 minutes of exercise, the body falls back on its energy reserves by burning fat.

A concentration of lactate above 4 mmol acts as a signal that the energy is now being provided anaerobically from carbohydrates.

Increased activity in the body also leads to an increased heart rate (pulse). By measuring the heart beat (pulse rate) and the blood lactate levels during sporting activity, it is possible to determine the pulse rate at which aerobic metabolism switches over to anaerobic metabolism. The athlete can then learn exactly how to control his pulse rate in training and in competition, according to whether he wishes to be in a state of aerobic or anaerobic metabolism.

The performance testing which is carried out in sports medicine centres serves to determine these parameters.

5.2 What is performance testing?

During a performance test the sports scientist can use the readings from an exercise bicycle or treadmill to determine at which intensity levels the athlete is still producing energy aerobically, and also the level at which the oxygen breathed in is no longer sufficient for proper fat-burning (anaerobic metabolism). To do this the heart rate (beats per minute) and lactate concentrations (lactic acid in the blood) are measured as the intensity is gradually increased in stages. Heart rate and lactate concentrations give information about current activity in the body, and a correlation of the two parameters gives an indication of the individual capabilities. Together with a general sports fitness examination this can uncover hidden illnesses, which could limit or forbid sporting activity.

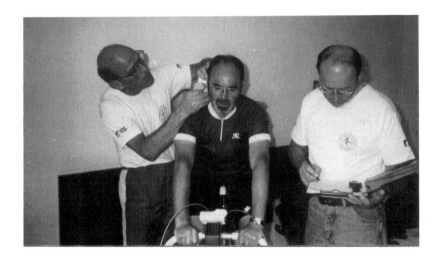

Diag. 175:
Taking blood samples from an athlete's earlobe during lactate testing.

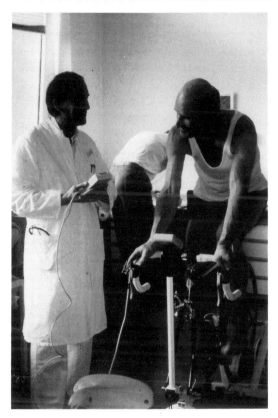

Diag. 176:
Ergometric bicycle test in a sports medicine centre in order to carry out a performance assessment for an endurance athlete.

Performance testing
Performance testing gives the *average athlete* information about his current state of health and highlights the areas of sporting activity to which he is best suited. *Elite athletes* use such specific sports medicine tests to determine their maximal degree of physical resilience and to gain recommendations as to how their training should proceed. Regular tests enable progress in training to be well-documented.

5.3   What Can the Athlete Derive from the Performance Test Results?

1. An athlete seeking general fitness will be able to use this knowledge to prevent overstraining the body and avoid damaging health to an extent where one would no longer be able to carry out one's sport.

2. The average athlete learns at which heart frequency (pulse rate) he is operating aerobically, when he is operating both aerobically and anaerobically and when he is relying exclusively on anaerobic metabolism. In endurance based sports he can use this to divide his energy equally over the whole period of training (duration of the competition), and can use the knowledge to determine personally the intensity at different phases of the competition.

3. The elite athlete can use repeated performance testing to determine his current state of fitness, and achieve improved conditioning while judging the training effect more precisely. This helps him to peak more precisely for the main focus of the season.

Performance Testing

Surname:	xxxxxxx		Club:		
First Name:	xxxxx		D.O.B.:	**25.8.57**	
Address:					

Resting pulse: **60**   Recovery pulse: 3 mins: **125**   5 mins: **120**

RE =	Recovery zone	below 1 mmol	120 – 160
BE =	Basic endurance zone	1 - 2 mmol	160 – 170
AT =	Aerobic tempo runs	2 - 4 mmol	170 – 188
PZ =	Progress zone (interval training)	3 - 5 mmol	180 – 193

HR   Lactate   Speed
(1/min) (mmol/l)   (km/h)

Speed in km/h
Heart rate
•••••• Lactate levels
– – – – 4 mmol lactate threshold

Time (mins)

Table 5:

Biological parameters determined from the treadmill tests enable a table to be drawn up. Important training zones for the runner can be determined from the relationship between pulse rates and blood lactate levels at increasing speeds.

5.4 What Are the Consequences of this Biological Data for the Runner?

1. For endurance training, training of more than an hour must be carried out every so often. Training (or competition) of this length should be carried out at low intensity (during aerobic metabolism), in order to give the body the opportunity to adjust to the training load, to mobilise the fat metabolism and thus delay a premature onset of fatigue in the body.

2. If the intention is to reduce body weight through sporting activity one should bear in mind that less intensive, but prolonged endurance training through mobilising the fat metabolism, brings more reward than shorter intensive training which burns the carbohydrate reserves without making an impression on the body fat reserves.

3. Interval training in the aerobic-anaerobic mixed zone not only improves the oxygen uptake ability, but also the capabilities at lower heart rates, and above all slows the increase in lactate levels.

Diag. 177:
After the test the results are evaluated by the computer and immediately discussed with the athlete.

5.5   Training Guidance

The leading criterion used to guide training biologically is the constant monitoring of the heart rate (pulse) during running. For this a heart rate monitor is needed. The exact ECG frequency is measured by a chest band (sender) and transmitted to the heart rate monitor on the wrist (receiver, computer and indicator).
(Diags. 178 and 179)

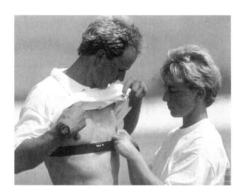 

Diag. 178-179:
The heart rate can be transmitted without wires from a chest band (sender) to the heart rate monitor watch displayed on the wrist, and can be continually controlled and monitored during running. Hence the runner knows exactly which training zone he is training in and his current metabolic state. (Polar Elektro GmbH)

The different training zones (intensity and duration) are determined for each individual training session by the athlete or coach according to the biological data provided by the performance tests.

Comfortable heart rate monitors can also have a 'memory' function. This makes it possible to carry out a digital or computer steered exact analysis of the accuracy and efficiency of the session.

The analysis can examine the whole training period or just certain sections. (see following tables)

Diag. 180:
The training session can be analysed using a PC and interface.

Tables 6-11:
By plotting the heart rate curve the training session or competition can be analysed in sections. The amount of time the body spent in the individual heart rate zones can then be displayed in a block diagram (right hand side of the graph).

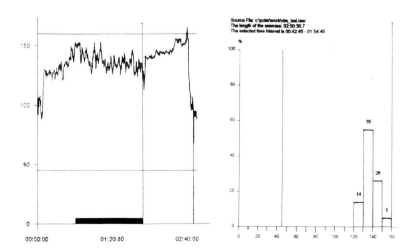

A: Cycling training during a short triathlon (1.5 – 40 – 10 km)

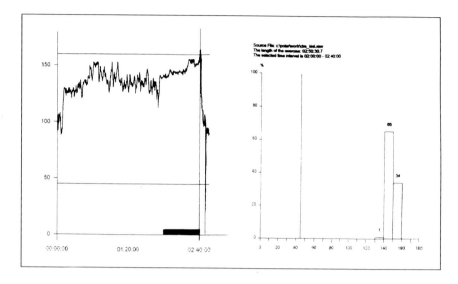

B: Running section of the triathlon

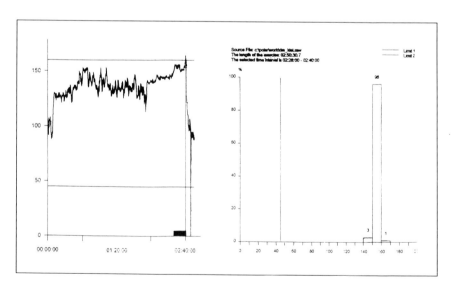

C: Finishing spurt

5.6   Analysing Competitions

Example 1:
1. Known data:

Metabolic zone	Heart rate (beats/min)
Aerobic zone	up to 150
Aerobic/anaerobic zone	up to 165
Anaerobic zone	above 170

2. Aim:
23 km mountainous run on the Nuremberg Ring with occasional inclines of up to 17%. Planned target of under two hours. The first hour should be run in the aerobic metabolic zone and thereafter in the aerobic/anaerobic mixed zone. The tempo should be raised over the last two kilometres until the anaerobic zone is entered, as far as strength allows.

3. Course of events:

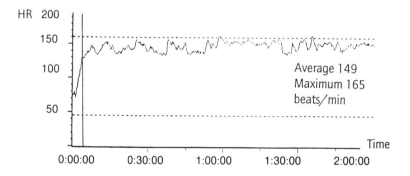

4. Comments:
After an hour of running in the aerobic metabolic zone the tempo was picked up to enter the aerobic/anaerobic mixed region. After 25 minutes of slightly increased effort the tempo slowed just enough so that the athlete was running in the upper aerobic zone once again. The aim: to complete the competition in under two hours was not achieved. The reason probably lay in faulty planning, which was thought out for a flat race and not a mountainous run.

Example 2:
1. Known data:

Metabolic zone	Heart rate (beats/min)
Aerobic zone	**up to 130**
Aerobic/anaerobic zone	**up to 140**
Anaerobic zone	**above 140**

2. Aim:
Ironman-Triathlon in Roth, 1993 (3.8 – 180 – 42.2 km). To improve on the previous year's competition time.

3. Course of events:

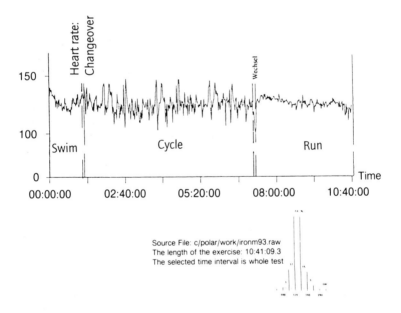

Source File: c/polar/work/ironm93.raw
The length of the exercise: 10:41:09.3
The selected time interval is whole test

4. Comments:
The competition went to perfectly to plan. 64% of the heart rate was in the aerobic zone. The previous year's competition time was improved by 34 min with the help of biologically planned competition tactics despite a reduced volume of training over the year.

Conclusions

"Optimise Your Running" does not only mean improving the individual achievements and capabilities, but also doing this whilst remaining practically injury free. The antithesis to this is that many biological and currently performance limiting conditions can arise from increased training of the wrong type, these can lead to overuse injuries, often necessitating a complete break from training.

The first problems experienced during long-distance running or afterwards can have various causes. Usually it is a case of an overburdening due to training errors, incorrect use of sporting machinery or faulty equipment. The first signs of an overburdening do not immediately mean medical disturbances requiring professional treatment. Only after the original mistakes have been repeated and the problem ignored can it lead to a proper illness or injury.

He who takes a break from training at the first sign of an overburdening problem has a good chance that the irritated condition of the tendons, the bursa or the muscles will subside after a few days. However, a certain predisposition towards renewed overstraining or irritation remains for several weeks, hence the affected part of the body clearly needs to be subjected to reduced stress loads for this period. This does not however mean that the athlete can continue straight on with his training as soon as the first signs of overburdening have subsided. He must begin to build up his training slowly and cautiously at first, particularly where the affected tendons or muscle groups are involved, in order to avoid gradually increasing the problem once again. Athletes often see the interruption of the scheduled training – often even in the precompetition phase – leading to a spiralling of their problems and fear that the goals for which they have worked, and even slaved over, for months will float away. Yet impatience and overestimating the individual biological conditions, in such a situation can lead to a repeat of the overburdening and finally to overuse damage needing professional treatment and an essentially longer break from training.

However, when one understands that sport is a leisure activity, intended to maintain health and fitness, one is more likely to accept the need for an adequate break from training in the case of overburdening. Furthermore it is futile to try to work against nature and continue to train (eventually even with the help of a doctor) possibly risk unforeseen consequences which could result in a reduction in the quality of life. In extreme cases this can result in sporting activity having to be totally avoided.

This book has provided the runner with basic knowledge to enable him to accurately understand his own body and correctly recognise the most frequent overburdening problems in time to treat them with the recommended measures. Thus the athlete assumes responsibility for his own body and individual health.

Normally the athlete needs to try to maintain fitness and condition as far as possible when training is interrupted for many weeks. Alternative sports disciplines can be used to maintain strength, endurance and co-ordination. Cycling, above all, can help the runner to conserve strength and endurance in the leg muscles during ongoing problems. However if the knee joint is irritated than cycling is not recommended. In such cases cross-country skiing in winter and using rollerskis on firm ground in summer are better options.

Conscientious athletes will certainly have used this book to learn about their personal biological make-up. They will soon learn to respect the barriers of their capabilities. So equipped they will be able to enjoy their endurance sport for its originally intended purpose:

An enthusiastic sports person should not make running the centre of his life, but rather a pleasurable minor part of life. As a first class hobby endurance sports, and in particular running, can help those in sedentary professions to improve their physical well-being and increase their standard of living. In this way their life is enriched and at the same time their health is stabilised in the latter stages of life.

Further Reading

Ahonen, J./Laktinen, T./
Sandström, Re./
Pogliani, G./Wirhed, R.:

Sportmedizin und Trainingslehre
Schaltauer Verlag,
Stuttgart/New York, 1994.

Aschoff, J.B./Kramer, Günther K.:

Energiehaushalt und Thermoregulation. B.2.
In: Gauer/Kramer/Jung:
Physiologie des Menschen,
Urban & Schwarzberg Verlag,
München, 1971.

Brody, D.M./Netter, H.:

Running Injuries, Clinical.
Symposia-CIBA. Vol. 32
Nr. 4/1980.

Bürkle, H.:

Aktives Rückentraining.
Karlsruher Rückenforum
Gymnastik-Programm für die Wirbelsäule.

Diem, C.J./Hess, H.:

Der Laufschuhratgeber.
Sportinfo.
Verlag-Oberhaching, 1986.

Diem, C.J.:

Tips für Laufanfänger.
Meyer & Meyer Verlag, Aachen
4. Auflage 1999.

Diem, C.J.:

Testkriterien für Lauf- (Jogging-) Schuhe.
Sportverl.
In: Sportschäden, 7, 196-199, 1993.

Diem, C.J.:

Empfehlungen für den Laufschuh
Teil 1 und 2.
In: Triathlon & Duathlon Nr. 3+4
41-47 (1995).

Fixx, J. F.:

Das komplette Buch vom Laufen.
Deutsche Bearbeitung:
H. Obermann/H. Hess.
Wolfgang Krüger Verlag, Frankfurt/Main 1979.

Hottenrott, K./Urban, V.:

Handbuch für Skilanglauf.
Meyer & Meyer Verlag, Aachen 1996.

Kapandji, I. A.:

Funktionelle Anatomie der Gelenke. Band 2.
Enke Verlag, Stuttgart 1985.

Kleinmann, D.:

Laufen, Sportmedizinische Grundlagen,
Trainingslehre und Risikoprophylaxe.
Schattauer Verlag, Stuttgart/New York 1996.

Köhler, B./Reber, H.:

Kinder machen Fußgymnastik
Enke Verlag, Stuttgart 1985.

Körner, W./Blankenstein, G./
Dorsch, P./Reinehr, U.:

Dunova, eine saugfähige Synthesefaser für
hohen Tragekomfort.
In: Chemiefasern/Textilindustrie, Juni 1979,
Bd. 29 6/452-462.

Letuwnitz, S.:

Bodytrainer: 10 Varianten-Programm für eine
tolle Figur.
Rowohlt-Verlag, Reinbek 1993.

Lohrer, H.:

Die Achillessehne im Sport – ungeliebtes Krank-
heitsbild Achillodynie,
In: TW Sport und Medizin, 5, 377-381, 1992.

Lütte, J./Ziegler, R.:

Krankengymnastik im Wandel der Zeit.
Arthron-diagnostischer und therapeutischer
Mittelpunkt.
In: TW Sport+Medizin F, 4, 234-241 1995.

Marcinko, D.:

Hallux valgus
Ullstein-Mosby Verlag, Berlin 1994.

Marées, H. de: Sportphysiologie.
                                        8. korrigierte Neuauflage,
                                        Sport & Buch Strauß, Köln 1996.

Mecheels, J.:   Körper – Klima – Kleidung.
                                        Grundzüge der Bekleidungsphilosophie.
                                        Schiele & Schön Verlag, Berlin 1991.

Nigg, B./Seger, M.B.:   Orthopädische Anfordung und biomechanische
                                        Konzepte im Sportschuhbau.
                                        Aus: Der Schuh im Sport II, Luzern 1991.

Peterson-Kendell, F./   Muskelfunktionen und Test.
Kendell-Mc Creavy, E.:   G. Fischer Verlag, Stuttgart/New York 1985.

Pförringer, W./Ullmann, Ch.:   Radfahren, Touren, Rennen, Mountain Bike.
                                        Südwest Verlag, München 1990.

Ruck, H.:   Das Buch der Fußpflege.
                                        Verlag Haruck, Schönberg 1990.

Schaff, P.:   Biomechanische und orthopädische Probleme
                                        des Laufschuhs.
                                        Aus: Der Schuh im Sport II, Luzern 1991.

Schauwecker, F.:   Hüftgelenk, Bericht über Unfallmedizin
                                        Tagung in Mainz 12./13.11.1994.

Schimpf, A.:   Füße und Schuhe im Sport.
                                        Karhu Deutschland GmbH.

Schultz, W.:   Sport- und Überlastungsschäden beim Lauf.
                                        Maurer Verlag, Gerslingen 1988.

Segesser, B./Pfüringer, W.:   Der Schuh im Sport.
                                        Perimed Verlag, Erlangen 1987.

Spring, H./Kunz, HR./   Kraft.
Schneider, W./Tritscher, Th./Unold, E.: Georg Thieme Verlag, Stuttgart 1990.

Stacoff, A.:

Laufschuhe müssen auch Läufer führen.
In: Läufer, 8, 44-46, 1995.

Verlag Europa Lehrmittel – Noumey,
Vollmer GmbH & Co., Haan-Gruiten

„Fachwissen Bekleidung", 4. Auflage.

Weicker, H./Strobel, G.:

Sport-Medizin, Biochemisch-physiologische
Grundlagen und ihre sportartspezifische
Bedeutung.
Gustav Fischer Verlag, Stuttgart/Jena/New
York 1994.

Wessinghage, T.:

So machen Sie Ihre Füße fit.
In: Runners World, 10, 46-53, 1995.

Wirhed, R.:

Sportanatomie und Bewegungslehre.
2. Auflage,
Schattauer Verlag, Stuttgart 1988.

Our Programme

Jozef Sneyers
Soccer Training
An Annual Programme

ISBN 1-84126-017-7
c. DM 34 ,-/SFr 31,60/ÖS 248,-
£ 12.95/US$ 19.95
Austr.$ 29.95/Can$ 29.95

Gerhard Frank
Soccer Training Programmes

ISBN 3-89124-556-4
DM 29,80/SFr 27,70/ÖS 218,-
£ 12.95/US$ 17.95
Austr.$ 29.95/Can$ 25.95

Ilona E. Gerling
Teaching Children's Gymnastics

ISBN 3-89124-549-1
DM 29,80/SFr 27,70/ÖS 218,-
£ 12.95/US $ 17.95
Austr.$ 29.95/Can$ 25.95

Bischops/Gerards
Soccer ●
Warming-up and Cooling down

ISBN 1-84126-014-2
c. DM 24,80/SFr 23,-/ÖS 181,-
£ 8.95/US$ 14.95
Austr.$24.95/Can$ 20.95

Bischops/Gerards
Junior Soccer:
A Manual for Coaches

ISBN 1-84126-000-2
DM 29,80/SFr 27,70/ÖS 218,-
£ 12.95/US$ 17.95
Austr.$ 29.95/Can$ 25.95

Thomas Kaltenbrunner
Contact Improvisation

ISBN 3-89124-485-1
DM 29,80/SFr 27,70/ÖS 218,-
£ 12.95/US$ 17.95
Austr.$ 29.95/Can$ 25.95

Bischops/Gerards
Soccer ●
One-On-One

ISBN 1-84126-013-4
c. DM 24,80/SFr 23,-/ÖS 181,-
£ 8.95/US$ 14.95
Austr.$24.95/Can$ 20.95

Bischops/Gerards
Coaching Tips for Children's Soccer

ISBN 3-89124-529-7
DM 14,80/SFr 14,40/ÖS 108,-
£ 5.95/US$ 8.95
Austr.$ 14.95/Can$ 12.95

Dörte Wessel-Therhorn
Jazz Dance Training

ISBN 3-89124-499-1
DM 29,80/SFr 27,70/ÖS 218,-
£ 12.95/US$ 17.95
Austr.$ 29.95/Can$ 25.95

Gerhard Frank
Soccer ●
Creative Training

ISBN 1-84126-015-0
c. DM 24,80/SFr 23,-/ÖS 181,-
£ 8.95/US$ 14.95
Austr.$24.95/Can$ 20.95

Pieter/Heijmans
Scientific Coaching for Olympic Taekwondo

ISBN 3-89124-389-8
DM 29,80/SFr 27,70/ÖS 218,-
£ 12.95/US$ 17.95
Austr.$ 29.95 Can$ 25.95

Bergmann/Butz
Adventure Sports – Big Foot

ISBN 3-89124-497-5
DM 34 ,-/SFr 31,60/ÖS 248,-
£ 14.95/US$ 19.95
Austr.$ 29.95/Can$ 29.95

Erich Kollath
Soccer ●
Techniques & Tactics

ISBN 1-84126-016-9
c. DM 24,80/SFr 23,-/ÖS 181,-
£ 8.95/US$ 14.95
Austr.$24.95/Can$ 20.95

Rudolf Jakhel
Modern Sports Karate

ISBN 3-89124-428-2
DM 29,80/SFr 27,70/ ÖS 218,-
£ 12.95/US$ 17.95
Austr.$ 29.95/Can$ 25.95

Münch/ Mund
Straight Golf

ISBN 3-89124-503-3
DM 34,-/SFr 31,60/ÖS 248,-
£ 12.95/US$ 19.95
Austr.$ 29.95/Can$ 25.95

● Publication date: Fall 1999/Spring 2000

MEYER
& MEYER
SPORT

Our Programme

Hömberg/Papageorgiou
Handbook for Beach-Volleyball

ISBN 3-89124-322-7
DM 38,-/SFr 35,30/ÖS 278,-
£ 17.95/US$ 29.-
Austr.$ 37.95/Can$ 39.95

Neumann/Pfützner/ Berbalk
Successful Endurance Training ●

ISBN 1-84126-004-5
DM 34 ,-/SFr 31,60/ÖS 248,-
£ 12.95/US$ 17.95
Austr.$ 29.95/Can$ 29.95

Richard Schönborn
Advanced Techniques for Competitive Tennis

ISBN 3-89124-534-3
DM 38.-/SFr 35,30/ÖS 278,-
£ 17.95/US$ 29.-
Austr. $ 37.95/Can $ 39.95

Papageorgiou/Spitzley
Volleyball:
A Handbook for Coaches and Players

ISBN 1-84126-005-3
DM 34 ,-/SFr 31,60/ÖS 248,-
£ 14.95/US$ 19.95
Austr.$ 29.95/Can$ 29.95

Kuno Hottenrott
The Complete Guide to Duathlon Training

ISBN 3-89124-530-0
DM 34 ,-/SFr 31,60/ÖS 248,-
£ 14.95/ US$ 19.95
Austr.$ 29.95/Can$ 29.95

Lutz Steinhöfel
Training Exercises for Competitive Tennis

ISBN 3-89124-464-9
DM 29,80/SFr 27,70/ÖS 218,-
£12.95/US$ 17.95
Austr.$ 29.95/Can$ 25.95

Georg Neumann
Nutrition in Sport ●

ISBN 1-84126-003-7
c. DM 34 ,-/SFr 31,60/ ÖS 248,-
£ 12.95/US$ 17.95
Austr.$ 29.95/Can$ 29.95

Hermann Aschwer
The Complete Guide to Triathlon Training

ISBN 3-89124-515-7
DM 34 ,-/SFr 31,60/ÖS 248,-
£ 12.95/US$ 19.95
Austr.$ 29.95/Can$ 29.95

Dieter Koschel
Allround Fitness
The Beginner's Guide

ISBN 1-84126-011-8
DM 24,80/SFr 23,-/ÖS 181,-
£ 9.95/US $ 14.95
Austr.$ 24.95/Can$ 20.95

Bös/Saam
Walking
Fitness and Health through Everyday Activity

ISBN 1-84126-001-0
DM 14,80/SFr 14,40/ÖS 108,-
£ 5.95/US$ 8.95
Austr.$ 14.95/Can$ 12.95

Achim Schmidt
Handbook of Competitive Cycling

ISBN 3-89124-509-2
DM 34 ,-/SFr 31,60/ÖS 248,-
£ 12.95/US$ 19.95
Austr.$ 29.95/Can$ 29.95

Bettina M. Jasper
Train your Brain

Mental and Physical Fitness

ISBN 3-89124-531-9
DM 29,80/SFr 27,70/ÖS 218,-
£12.95/US$ 17.95
Austr.$ 29.95/Can$ 25.95

Petracic/Röttgermann/Traenckner
Successful Running

ISBN 1-84126-006-1
DM 24,80/SFr 23,-/ÖS 181,-
£ 9.95/US$ 14.95
Austr.$ 24.95/Can$ 20.95

Achim Schmidt
Mountainbike Training

ISBN 1-84126-007-X
DM 29,80/SFr 27,70/ÖS 218,-
£ 12.95/US$ 17.95
Austr.$ 29.95/Can$ 25.95

Uwe Rheker
Integration through Games and Sports

ISBN 1-84126-012-6
DM 29,80/SFr 27,70/ÖS 218,-
£ 12.95/US $ 17.95
Austr.$ 29.95/Can $ 25.95

MEYER & MEYER SPORT

e-mail: verlag@meyer-meyer-sports.com • **Please order by:** www.meyer-meyer-sports.com

Please order our catalogue!

IAAF/
Gert-Peter Brüggemann (ed.)
Biomechanical Research Project

ISBN 1-84126-009-6
DM 39,80/SFr 37,-/ÖS 291,-
£ 15.-/US$ 24.-
Austr.$ 37.95/Can$ 39.95

Maurice Roche (ed.)
CSRC Edition Volume 5
Sport, Popular Culture and Identity

SBN 3-89124-468-1
DM 29,80/SFr 27,70/ÖS 218,-
£ 12.95/US $ 17.95
Austr.$ 29.95/Can$25.95

SLPE Volume 3
Merkel/ Tokarski (eds.)
Racism and Xenophobia in European Football

ISBN 3-89124-343-X
DM 29,80/SFr 27,70/ÖS 218,-
£ 12.95/US$ 17.95
Austr.$ 29.95/Can$ 25.95

---

de Knop/ Theeboom/
van Puymbroeck (et. al.)
Recreational Games and Tournaments

ISBN 3-89124-446-0
DM 29,80/SFr 27,70/ÖS 218,-
£12.95/US$ 17.95
Austr.$ 29.95/Can$ 25.95

Sugden/Bairner (eds.)
CSRC Edition Volume 4
Sport in Divided Societies

ISBN 3-89124-445-2
DM 29,80/SFr 27,70/ÖS 218,-
£ 12.95/US $ 17.95
Austr.$ 29.95/Can$ 25.95

SLPE Volume 2
Doll-Tepper/Brettschneider(eds.)
Physical Education and Sport - Changes and Challenges

ISBN 3-89124-320-0
DM 39,80/ SFr 37,-/ÖS 291,-
£ 17.95/US$ 29.-
Austr.$37.95/Can$ 39.95

Green/Hardman (eds.)
Physical Education A Reader

ISBN 3-89124-463-0
DM 39,80/SFr 37,-/ÖS 291,-
£ 17.95/US $ 29,-
Austr.$ 37.95/ Can$ 39.95

Alan Tomlinson (ed.)
CSRC Edition Volume 3
Gender, Sport and Leisure

ISBN 3-89124-443-6
DM 34,-/SFr 31,60/ÖS 248,-
£ 14.95/US $ 24.-/ Austr. $
32.95/Can $ 34.95

SLPE Volume 1
Sport Sciences in Europe 1993 – Current and Future Perspectives

ISBN 3-89124-222-0
DM 39,80/SFr 37,-/ÖS 291,-
£ 17.95/US$ 29.-
Austr.$ 37.95/Can$ 39.95

Graham McFee (ed.)
CSRC Edition Volume 7
Dance, Education and Philosophy

ISBN 1-84126–008-8
DM 29,80/SFr 27,70/ÖS 218,-
£ 12.95/US$ 17.95
Austr.$ 29.95/Can$ 25.95

McFee/Tomlinson (eds.)
CSRC Edition Volume 2
Education, Sport and Leisure

ISBN 3-89124-442-8
DM 29,80/SFr 27,70/ÖS 218,-
£ 12.95/US $ 17.95
Austr.$ 29.95/Can$ 25.95

ISCPES
Hardman/ Standeven
Cultural Diversity and Congruence in PE and Sport

ISBN 3-89124-557-2
DM 39,80/ SFr 37,-/ÖS 291,-
£ 17.95/US$ 29.-
Austr.$37.95/Can$ 39.95

Lincoln Allison (ed.)
CSRC Edition Volume 6
Taking Sport Seriously

ISBN 3-89124-479-7
DM 29,80/SFr 27,70/ÖS 218,-
£ 14.95/US $ 17.95
Austr.$ 28.95/Can$ 25.95

Tomlinson/Fleming (eds.)
CSRC Edition Volume 1
Ethics, Sport and Leisure

ISBN 3-89124-441-X
DM 34,-/SFr 31,60/ÖS 248,-
£ 14.95/US $ 24.-
Austr. $ 32.95/Can $ 34.95

ICSSPE/ The Multidisciplinary Series of Physical Education and Sport Science / **Volume 1**
Perspectives

ISBN 1-84126-019-3
c. DM 29,80/SFr 27,70/ÖS 218
£14.95/US$ 19.95
Austr.$ 29.95/Can$ 29.95

Meyer & Meyer Sport • Von-Coels-Str. 390 • D-52080 Aachen • Fax: 0049241/9 58 10 10

MEYER & MEYER SPORT

THE AUTHORS

A private lecturer with a doctorate in medicine and science, *Dr. Bozo Petračić,* has been Head Doctor at St. Clemens Hospital, Oberhausen-Sterkrade since 1983. An active marathon runner and triathlete, he was a founder member of the Oberhausen Association of Sports Doctors.

Franz-Joachim Röttgermann is an independent Orthopaedic Foot Specialist and runs a clinic to deal with foot and leg related gait problems in athletes. He is himself an active endurance athlete.

Dr-Ing. Kurt-Christian Traenckner, Dipl-Chem., studied Chemistry and Fuel Technology. Professionally he has worked in various fields in the Mining and Chemical Industries. As an endurance athlete he currently also dedicates himself to Sports Medicine.